VIOLENCE
IN THE
CITY

Norma Iris Pagan Morales

ISBN 978-1-959895-60-2 (paperback)
ISBN 978-1-959895-59-6 (ebook)

Printed in the United States of America

Acknowledgement

This book is dedicated to police officers all around the world. Thank you for your service.

Overview

Qualities of a Police Officer

Police Officers are the most trusted authorities of society. They help others without thinking about their life. They must face different problems while helping us. Still, they never hesitate, and this encourage young adults to become police officers.

Some major qualities of police are:

They help everyone rich or poor. They never discriminate against people for money.

They have the power to catch the criminals, and this develops a positive attitude in society because people fear of being caught when they do something wrong or illegal.

They never hesitate to handle any case because they are brave and courageous.

Introduction

Every country has its own rules and regulations, and these rules are made to maintain harmony in the country.

Sometimes people neglect the rule and do some unwanted things and others get disturbed. So, to have an eye on the society government made police. Police are the government bodies that maintain peace in society. They help people in different ways and never let people face any difficulty.

The Importance of a Police Officer

A police officer has many responsibilities, one side they must maintain peace in the society and the other side they also must catch the criminals. If the crime rate increases in a particular area, then they must answer the higher authorities. Police are not those who remain in a police station and write your report. They also ought to solve many cases and some unsolved murder mysteries.

They must be smart, brave, clever, and focused at the same time because a single mistake can keep the matter unsolved. Really, they are the real heroes. Many of us say, that it's a duty of the police to maintain peace in society and decrease the crime rates.

In my opinion, one should also try his best and cooperate with the police officers. We live in society, and one should always keep his eyes open when he/she is out from home.

How to Cooperate with Police Officer

When you step out of the house always be careful. Sometimes a chain snatcher or a purse snatcher can attack you. Instead of cursing the police one should be alert on road. You know that the police cannot be present everywhere, there are more than 135 crore people in India, and it is not possible to provide security to each one.

Sometimes police can stop you and ask you a few things, so never obstruct their work and cooperate with them, because sometimes it is necessary to have some details regarding any case. So, rather misbehaving and arguing, respect them and answer them.

One of the most important things is to follow the rules, if the government has made certain rule please follow. You never know how difficult and annoying it is for the police, to always make sure that you are wearing a helmet. It is just for your safety; they make sure that everyone follows the rule.

Be a true citizen, suppose you see someone doing anything wrong just knock them. Being a citizen of the country, you also have equal rights to raise your voice against anything wrong. Nowadays people wait for the police and start making videos. Instead of making videos and posting it on social media, help others and the police at your level.

How Police Helps People

I don't think I can mention all their duties and work in one book, but I will try my best to show the responsibilities of the police.

Contents

Chapter 1

Crime in the Big Apple

This is a serious situation that can happen to anyone. Police Officer John Anderson of the 5th Pct, in New York City. He is the narrator of this tale. He is trying to write a statement about an incident that occurred in his precinct.

Sometimes it is critical when we become angry, and that anger turns into mobilized actions designated to eliminate crime and disorder problems that terrorize the safety of any community.

When news of the terrorist attacks reached me, I was working on the piece that follows. It is the story of a single act of aggression inflicted by a police officer on the body of a citizen.

In the day, as the series of act of violence became apparent, it seemed a treat to concentrate on arranging words on a page.

To write a report on this incident, I really had a hard time. I even lost my thoughts.

Many have observed the events of September 11th, 2001, in their own way. It has changed everything. Perhaps it would be more accurate to say that they disclosed the underlying terms of existence. As a survivor of violence once observed.

Two weeks have now passed. New York City remains covered with ashes. The aftershock continues to unsettle our lives. Thousands of tragic individuals narrate experiences and their sufferings.

They spoke in detail about their tragic. The testimonies were endless. It was hard for any of them to deal with so much grief.

During much confusion, this much is clear: violence is prepared in the domain of words before it is inscribed on the bodies of human beings.

Consider what had to happen in the semantic realm for those who planned and executed mass murder on September 11th to be capable of such acts.

Our national efforts to come to terms with what happened on the 11th. The fates of whole populations now turn on the choices we make between words, on the metaphors we adopt, on the stories we tell.

As The New York Times resumes publication, we rededicate ourselves to the work on resisting violence wherever we encounter it, and in whatever form, by using language responsibly to call things by their true names.

In that spirit, we offer the following report:

One in an ongoing series on police violence in public housing located on the Delancey section of New York City sometimes called by some "Alphabet City".

On the morning of Thursday, September 6th, Ray Brown went to buy some cigarettes, a 45-year-old resident of New York City. Brown was visiting a friend who lives in 5419 Avenue C, in the housing projects. He descended by way of the stairs because the elevators, as is often the case, were not working.

The open-air lobbies of the "Delancey building," as residents refer to is the setting for an active drug marketplace. It is also the scene of much other activity.

The residents are always coming and going throughout the day. One can see children with brightly colored knapsacks heading out to school in the morning and returning in the afternoon. There were friends enjoying each other's company in pleasant public space.

Even when stepping out for just a few minutes, Brown makes a point of taking his wallet containing identification, because he has been stopped by police who threatened him and charged him with criminal trespass.

He also carries a letter signed by his friend which states that he is on the development for the purpose of visiting her.

Brown bought some cigarettes three for a dollar from one of the men in the building then chatted with friends.

As Brown was talking to his friends, the police appeared out of nowhere. There were five unmarked cars and a police wagon. They were looking for drug dealers. The dealers fled upstairs. The community members in the vicinity began to disperse.

When Brown saw the police, he returned to the lobby... He remembered very clear that he walked away. He didn't run. He walked at a normal pace. His only intention was to pass through the lobby, out the other side to go to the store.

"I got halfway past the mailboxes, " he recalled, "and that's the last thing I remember. I woke up spitting teeth."

According to witnesses, a plainclothes police officer ran up behind Brown and hit him with full force in the back. It was with something that resembled a baseball bat. The impact slammed him face first to the ground and sent his body skidding forward some fifteen feet.

"It was," a witness said of the sound, "like an egg hitting the ground and smashing." Brown was blind-sided. He had no warning that the blow was coming. The officer said nothing prior to striking him. "He didn't say, 'I'm an officer.' He didn't say, 'Stop!' He didn't say anything."

Witnesses said that the officer's name is Thomas Di Angelo. Everyone knows Di Angelo because he is a corrupted and enjoys abusing his power as a police officer.

Brown passed out briefly. He lay face down on the concrete. His nose was broken. His two top front teeth were knocked out and driven through his upper lip.

"I sat up on the ground, trying to compose myself. Another plainclothes police officer said, 'Get your black ass up. There isn't anything wrong with you. Get your black ass up.' I rolled over and got on my knees.

As I was getting up, he grabbed my arm and slammed me up against the wall."

This police officer took him to the police wagon where they were collecting dozens of people they had arrested. As far as Brown knows, he was the only one they roughed up.

He was bleeding freely. He overheard the sergeant at the door of the police wagon say, "Get him out of here." They took him to the paramedics.

The paramedic who treated him was very nice. He took him outside to find his two front teeth in the hope that they could be restored.

Brown had been unconscious, therefore, the paramedic insisted that he must be taken to the hospital to be examined.

The ambulance took him to Bellevue Hospital. He was accompanied by two uniformed officers. "They were really nice, stated Brown. They said they couldn't understand why Police Officer Di Angelo did that to me."

After he was examined at Bellevue, he was taken to the police station. When he entered the station, he heard "some smart remarks like 'You won't try to run from the police no more, will you?'" But he also observed a good deal of uneasiness about his condition. "There were a lot of mixed emotions down at that police station."

He saw the officer who slammed him to the ground. "I asked him, 'Why did you do that to me?' He didn't say anything. He just walked off."

While waiting to be booked, Brown overheard discussion among the police about whether they should give him another charge resisting arrest or selling drugs. He also heard an exchange in which "they were trying to get someone other than the one that assaulted me to sign the police report."

4

He is not sure what the outcome was. At the end, he was charged with criminal trespass and solicitation of unlawful business.

He was taken to Central Booking at One Police Plaza where he spent the night. In pain from his injuries, he was unable to sleep. He was released on his own recognition on Friday morning and returned to Delancey's Housing Projects.

"Out of my forty-something years, this has never happened to me," Brown observed. "They want to categorize and put everybody in the same boat."

In telling his story, he took pains not to do the same with respect to the police. He didn't to put them all in the same boat. "All police are not bad." He recalled the solicitude of the two officers who took him to the hospital and the comments of others who were offended by what was done to him.

"Me myself, I don't bother anybody. I treat the police with the utmost respect. If they ask me a question, I answer them. If they tell me to go over there, I go over there. If they tell me to sit down, I sit down. But Police Officer Di Angelo assaulted me to the fullest and thought nothing of it."

Police Officer Anderson thought about the incident. He sees these cases day in and day out. Brown vs. Di Angelo case was treated fair.

Police Officer Thomas Di Angelo was terminated from the police force. He was sentenced to a five-year sentence for assaulting a citizen. He had other cases pending; therefore, he lost his police pension.

Chapter 2

No Backup

I am retired Detective Michael Mc Donald and the story you are about to read is true. As you read you will be more knowledgeable of the work of a police officer.

During the first several years that I worked as a police officer, I was assigned to the 25 Precinct. That precinct is in Spanish Harlem, in New York City.

My partner was Police Officer Raymond Martinez. We learned to handle many types of calls by ourselves just because there were many times a back-up was not available. Sometimes your back-up was twenty or thirty miles away.

It would be nice to think that the public, the people you are trying to help, would come to your aid, but you quickly learn that all too often they won't lift a hand to help.

There are people out there who will go out of their way to help an officer, but they seem to be few and far between. It appears that a lot of people feel that officers are paid to take the risks and they aren't paid to get hurt trying to assist the Police.

This may be true, but the officer sees it as just another example of how the public doesn't care about any law enforcement. There is a wall between the officers and the people.

For the public, a police officer gets paid for their protection....

One evening, I received a disturbance call from 96 Street and 5th Avenue. The neighbors called and said it sounded like a fight was going on next door. There were about twenty duplex units in this complex.

It was early evening and when I arrived, and I found about half the residents outside in their yards watching what was going on. Police Officer Martinez was busy at the precinct, so I proceeded on my own. I thought that I would go and investigate. It was just a disturbance call....

I could hear shouting coming from the unit I had been sent to. I approached the apartment knowing that my back-up would not arrive for at least ten minutes, due to this location at the time of the call.

The door flew open as I got about twenty feet from it. A man in his early twenties, about my size, came out. He walked as if he was going for a walk. I told him that I wanted to talk to him.

He said something to the effect that he didn't want to talk to me. He was still about five feet from me when a girl came out of the apartment. She was crying and bleeding from the nose and mouth. She pointed at the man and stated that he had beaten her up and busted up her apartment.

The man was even with me by this time and still walking. I held out my hand to stop him and told him I wanted to talk to him. He pushed me and started running. He headed straight toward a group of about ten neighbors who were out in the street watching the show.

They parted like the Red Sea as he got to them. They were shouting for me to get him, but that was as much support as they were willing to give me.

I caught him in the middle of the street and told him he was under arrest. He took a swing at me, and we struggled for a minute or so. He was trying to get away and I was trying to get his arms behind him.

I lost my grip, and he took off running again. I ran him down this time in the front yard of the duplex across the street. Again, there were people all around us. They acted like this was all a game. I heard a lot of laughing and cheering. We struggled again. After a few minutes, he broke free and ran away from me.

I was angry by this time and tired of playing around. I caught him as he was about to go around the corner of the building, but this time instead of grabbing him I did a flying tackle on him from behind. There was a large rose bush in front of us and he landed in the middle of it with me on top of him. I managed to knock the fight out of him. I handcuffed him while he lay there. I wasn't going to give him a chance to run again.

Both of us had blood on our faces and arms from the thorn pricks. As we walked toward the patrol car the people just laughed. They were in a very festive mood. Some of them were clapping and cheering. They may not have cheered so loud if they had known what I thought of all the help they had given me.

My back-up arrived as I was putting my prisoner in the back of my patrol car. Even though everything was over, it surely was good to see another cop.

Chapter 3

Domestic Disturbances

This case is about a domestic dispute which goes bad and gets worse in court:

Many police officers have been hurt or killed while handling domestic disputes. They are all very dangerous situations and police officers must be ready to react quickly...

During domestic disturbances, people want the police officers to be referees. They know we will step in if things get too hot. They use this as a chance to say or do things they would not normally say to their spouse. Very often this will lead to an explosive situation. The police officers are not always aware of what is going on until it is too late.

Sometimes one will hear the call over the radio and recognizes the names. You get to know the couples. They make a pattern of getting drunk and then start a dispute.

This couple, Juanita, and Henry have been having domestic troubles for many years. We were very close to the location than any other patrol car. I told my partner that we can handle it, and that we still must call for a backup.

We arrived at the house, and as we got out of the patrol car, we saw two other officers coming down the street. We waited for them. They arrived and we walked up to the house.

The Henry opened the front door, and we stepped inside. The door opened into the living room. Straight ahead of us was a console television against the wall to our right. The rest of the living room spread out ahead of us and to our left. The couple had three children from about seven years old to a girl of fifteen. The children lived with their father, in this house. The mother had moved out.

Once we were inside, Henry said he wanted his Julie removed from the residence. I asked him what was going on. He stated that he had custody of the children. His wife had come to pick them up for the weekend. They had all gone out for supper together. During supper they had a couple of drinks and one thing lead to another.

By the time they got back to the house, they were arguing. Henry held out what he said was a restraining order stating that until their case got to court neither of them was to bother the other one.

The paper in his hand was ripped into little pieces. Henry said that Juanita had ripped it up when he called for an officer. I told him it didn't matter whether the paper was ripped or not because I was not going to try to enforce it. Restraining orders are tricky in the best of situations. In this case, they had both violated it by going out for supper together...

I told both that restraining orders were made to keep people apart so trouble would not start. I told them if the wife was going to take the children for the weekend, why not take them and leave, that would resolve the whole situation.

Juanita informed me that she could not leave because Henry had taken the coil off her car. The car needs that coil to run. I asked him about this, but he stated that it was a lie.

Our hopes of resolving this dispute quickly had faded. We told them both that we would listen to their stories one at a time starting with the wife. She started out with the same old thing about how they had not been able to make their marriage work.

Juanita said that her husband was a bum and a loser. While she was talking, she was standing in front of the console television facing me. Henry was standing to my left beside her. My partner had been standing behind me. Two more officers were outside. My partner stepped outside to let the other know that everything is going fine and that they may leave.

In the house there was a dog. We kept looking at it because dogs are trained to keep their eyes on their masters. They become very upset when they can't see them for a few minutes.

The front door had been open, but a screen door kept the dog from seeing his master. The officer stepped out and called the dog to be quiet. He had been barking and becoming more upset as time went by.

The officer stepped out because everything seemed under control. About the time he got out the door Juanita said, "And he's mad because he's afraid when we get to court, I'll say something about him having sex with his own fifteen-year-old daughter!"

I looked up from my notebook as Henry caught her with a right hook to the jaw which knocked her sideways onto the television. I dropped my flashlight, pen, and notebook as he jumped on her and grabbed her around the neck.

I shouted for the other officer and at the same time I grabbed the husband. I pulled him off her. My partner was just opening the screen door coming to help me, but he wasn't coming quickly enough for me. I threw the man out the door at him.

They both landed in a heap on the concrete steps. I dove on top of the heap. My partner had been caught off guard but reacted quickly. He grabbed the man from behind. He wrapped one arm over the man's shoulder and around his neck, with the other arm he tried to grab hold of the man's right arm. I tried to get both his arms so I could handcuff him. I heard the other officer scream. I looked up to see what was going on.

The man had the officer's hand in his mouth and was biting it. I slammed my fist into his stomach as hard as I could. He released his bite.

During all this, the six-year-old boy was running around smacking me. He was yelling for us to leave his daddy alone.

After several more minutes of struggling, we were able to get Henry handcuffed and under control. We also located the coil to Juanita's car under the seat of his truck. We put it back on her car. We also made sure she was not hurt. We then took the Henry to the precinct. We arrested him for assault and battery and resisting arrest.

The assault and battery charge went before the local Magistrate and the resisting arrest went to General Sessions court. The Magistrate court case came up first.

During the trial we called Juanita to the stand, but she told Judge Collins that she had provoked her husband and had deserved to be hit. She also told the Judge that we had no right to get involved because it was between the two of them.

The Judge Collins told her that it didn't matter what she thought. If her husband hit her and we saw it, we were right to charge him. The Judge found him guilty. It felt good to get the conviction, but it sure left a bad taste in my mouth.

We had to fight the man, get scraped and cut on the concrete, and my partner was bitten trying to protect a woman who wouldn't even help us in court...

This was just another hard lesson learned.

The result: Police Officers get colder, harder, and less caring because the public refuses to cooperate...

Chapter 4

Superheroes

This is a real superhero story...

In Bridgeport, Connecticut, School Resource Officer Carlos Carmo Jr. is being hailed a hero today. This, after footage was released showing him saving a group of kids.

Last month, Carmo was working the Harding High School Safe School Corridor as school was letting out.

Students were filing out into the sidewalks and crosswalks in Bridgeport's Boston Avenue as classes let out.

That's when a parked SUV began rolling downhill, headed into the busy street toward a traffic barrier and a group of students that were walking home.

Police say there was no driver inside of the car when it happened, but there were two passengers in it – including an elderly woman.

According to officials, the SUV somehow slipped out of park and rolled away.

According to police, as the runaway SUV began picking up speed, Officer Carmo sprang into action. In the screenshot below, you can see the SUV in the top right corner just miss a group about to cross at the crosswalk.

Using nothing more than his brute strength and friction, he completely stops it from rolling by dragging his feet along the pavement before it collided with anything or anyone.

During the maneuver, Officer Carmo reportedly sustained a few minor injuries. He was treated at the hospital and has since been released.

According to his superiors, he's now "being recognized for his bravery, selflessness and quick thinking in this emergency situation that could have been tragic had he not intervened."

In Hopewell, Virginia during the Thanksgiving holiday, a firefighter and mother of three was shot and killed on while trying to protect one of her children from stray bullets while they were walking outside.

Richmond fire Lieutenant Ashley Nicole Berry, 33, was enjoying the holiday at her boyfriend's family's home in Hopewell last week. According to reports, Berry was getting ready to leave the residence when someone suddenly started shooting at an apartment next to the home.

The shooting happened just before midnight. Hopewell Police Chief Kamran Afzal said investigators believe Berry was struck by a stray round as she tried to shield her five-year-old son from the gunfire.

Afzal made a statement to The Richmond Times-Dispatch about the events that played out:

"That's what I'd expect from [a first responder]. Firefighters and police officers give up their lives for other people and don't even think twice about it. She was not the intended target, and neither was the house where she was at. The apartment next to it was the target. She was at the wrong place at the wrong time … and got hit by a stray round."

Berry was transported to a local hospital with serious injuries, but was later transferred to VCU Medical Center, where she was pronounced dead shortly after arriving. Police stated the shooter looked to be in a gold or silver SUV that was seen speeding out of the area where Berry was shot.

Afzal was recently dubbed the police chief back in January, and this is the first time since his appointment that he's had to work a shooting case where "somebody who was not the intended target was killed".

Chapter 5

Nino

When I wrote this story, I was 45 years old. During that time, I've met and interacted with many people. Some I would classify as acquaintances, and others as friends.

There have been a few good friends, fewer, best friends. I can, however, tell you who was the best of the best of my friends; his name was Boston. I gave him that name. You see Nino was my dog. I say was, because unfortunately Boston is no longer among the living.

He met a violent ending. That's why I feel obligated to tell his story. Boston is dead, but I want his memory to live on. Not just in my mind, but with you who love your pets.

I may dramatize as I write of my Nino, but most will be telling you the truth.

When Nino and I first met, I was working for the city of New York Police Department. I was a police officer. I found an ad in the local paper from someone wanting a good home for a German shepherd pup.

I drove to the address I wrote down. As I pulled into the dirt drive and stared at the mobile home it reminded me of many of the homes I'd visited as a cop; run down and in need of repair. Indeed, in need of being torn down! The front yard was more dirt than grass. A few children's toys lie about: A wagon with three wheels, a tricycle with only one pedal. I looked at the windows, either without curtains or with home-made coverings.

I walked up the steps to the front door and knocked on the thin metal covering of its flimsy frame. I heard light footsteps from within, then the door opened.

I stared into the face of a woman, thirty to thirty-five, disheveled brown hair; a cigarette hanging loosely from her thin lips.

"Hi, I'm the one who called about the German Shepard pup."

The woman stared at me, her eyes going immediately to my shoes, then up. She then looked me in the eye: That's what makes women such good witnesses, and police officers'; they are so observant.

"Yes," she said. "My dog had several pups. They're all weaned now, and I just can't afford to feed them all."

"May I see them?"

"Sure. Please excuse the way the house looks; the kids tear it up faster than I can clean it."

I could see a dark-haired girl of about five peeking from behind the woman's tanned legs; exposed by cut-offs, cut way too high.

As she opened the door, a boy of about eight ran to a nearby couch, launching himself onto a cushion and sending up a dust cloud.

The woman led me to a room down the hall from the living room and cautiously opened the door, "Take your pick. Just keep the door closed so the rest don't get out."

I entered the room and was nearly overcome by the smell of dogs. The one window to the room was open but supplied little air, as hot humid summer currents entered it.

Opposite the door, on an old worn throw rug, were four pups. All but one cowered against the wall.

"Hey guys," I said in a low calming voice.

"Woof," was the reply from the one pup daring to challenge my entrance.

"I'm not going to hurt you," I said, as I slowly made my way to where the pups huddled.

Again, "Woof," came from the bold pup.

I stared at him. He was blacker than brown, typical Shepard markings; however, I found it hard to believe he was 'pure bred.'

I took a doggy treat from my shirt pocket, knelt, and offered it in the palm of my right hand. 'Mister adventure' slowly walked to my hand, smelled the morsel, and quickly snapped it up. I took a second snack out.

This time I put it in my left palm. The pup came to me a little faster this time. As he nosed toward the snack, I extended my right hand and softly stroked his thick coat. I saw his tail, curled over his back, start to wag.

"You're a lot huskier than your brothers and sisters. You remind me of a young lamb." I chose him. I will name him Nino.

When I left that day, Nino lay on the seat next to me. I left behind an authoritarian suggestion to either provide a cleaner living environment for the rest of the pups' or take them to the animal shelter. I reinforced this 'suggestion' by the purposeful disclosure of the badge I wore on my pant belt, usually hidden by my untucked tailed shirt.

As the days turned into weeks, and weeks into months, Nino and I closely bonded. My departure for work each evening found Nino staring out my living room window, his expression showing his displeasure that he was not going with me.

Early in the morning, when the rest of the world was sleeping, I would pull in the drive and see Nino's face at that same window; his mouth slightly opened, as if in a grin.

His body twitched with excitement as he bound for the door to meet me, tail wagging madly: Shrill yips coming from his growing lungs. Only after much petting, and a few of his favorite doggy treats, would he settle down; at my feet as I watched TV. If, while in my recliner, I slipped into sleep, I would awake to his body heat against my legs.

Nino and I shared long walks. I never gave Nino any formal training, but while on these walks I did make it a habit of keeping him on a tight leash at my left side.

There were two reasons for this. One, I wanted him to get used to staying near, not just straying all over. Second, I looked to the future of taking him on my 'beat.' If he were to walk with me while I was working, I wanted him on my left side; leaving my right side clear in case my weapon had to be drawn.

Working as a cop for the city of New York, I found myself working alone much of the time. Staten Island, a small borough, didn't have the budget for too many cops. There was a commander, a lieutenant, a couple of police officer.

The precinct had auxiliary officers. I was always alone. I dedicated most of my time, when not taking complaints, to providing an aggressive foot and mobile patrol. Except for the Chief, who had too many administrative duties to get out on the street much, the other officers' liked to work traffic enforcement. This of course was what the reserves' craved. Anyway, this worked out well for Nino and me.

After he was matured enough, I felt comfortable in bringing him to work with me. I wouldn't usually take Nino with me as I did my mobile patrol. I did take him on foot patrols.

It was during one of these foot patrols one summer night that Nino met some of the 'low life' his master had to deal with. I was working with a fellow full-time officer, Bill Ewald.

As Nino, Ewald and I walked down the sidewalk we came to the entrance to a restaurant. It was about 11:00 P.M. and the business was closed. Nino, as usual, was to my left and I was to Ewald's left, near the street: Farthest from the business entrance.

As we approached, I noticed two young men, in their late teens, early twenties, in the recessed doorway. I recognized both men: 'Scooter-bags.' That's my terminology for lowlife people that have no purpose in life, nor want one.

As Nino, Ewald and I passed by, one of the hoodlums remarked, "That dog bites me and I'll sue you."

That enraged me. Nino had done nothing to either man.

"Don't worry about the dog, it's his owner that bites," I replied.

A few weeks later I sat behind my desk at the precinct, typing a report. It was not uncommon for me to check out of service with the dispatchers after 3:00 A.M. and then, on my own time, catch up on reports.

Nino lies on the carpeted floor nearby, his head on his extended paws, his eyes closed. I knew he wasn't asleep; every minute or so he'd open his eyes, sometimes raise his head, look around and then lay his head down again.

The office I worked in was to the rear of the building. A nearby door led to the alleyway outside. I'd parked my van just off the alley, to the rear of the precinct.

As the keys to the typewriter, yes, in the 'old days' we used typewriters, clicked with each touch of my fingers I heard a low rumble coming from Nino's throat. The rumble turned to a growl.

"What's the matter Nino, someone out there?"

Nino kept his eyes on the door leading to the alley, his head now up; his ears reminded me of radar antenna: Both were standing straight but would rotate slightly every few seconds.

Nino didn't give false alarms, so I knew someone, or something, was outside the door. Nino stood up, his head cocked to one side, a short bark escaping his lips. I went for the door, unlocked it, and slowly turned the knob, wanting to only open the door slightly.

Suddenly, Nino launched himself at the small opening, forcing it open further, escaping into the darkness. Nino's shrill barks echoed in the alley as the sound of leather striking the pavement came to my ears.

"Get away! Get away!" Came a man's voice, somewhere down the alley.

"Nino!" I yelled, trying to get him to return.

I looked at my van, seeing my radio antenna bent at a 45-degree angle.

"Son-of-a-bitch! I hope Nino tears you a new ass hole," I yelled down the alley.

I stepped from the semi-darkness of where my van was parked, to the street-lit alleyway. I saw Nino returning, at a slow run.

The night air was humid, its currents bringing smells of decaying foodstuffs and stale beer from earlier activities at the nearby bar.

"Did you get him, Nino?" I asked, as I lowered myself on my thighs.

Nino came to me, his tail wagging. I found a dot of red on the end of his snout. I checked him over for injuries. There were none.

"Yep, you nailed him. Good boy," I said, reaching into my uniform shirt pocket for a doggy treat.

A couple of days later I stopped for gas, in my personal car. Frank Thomas, the 'scooter-bag' who'd said, "That dog bites me and I'll sue you," was inside the store when I went in.

Frank grabbed his soda from the counter and brushed past me, his eyes avoiding mine. Frank held the soda in his left hand. He had a bandage on his right hand.

Nino and I were real buddies. If I were late getting home, which I was many times, he was still glad to see me. If I were too busy to play with him some days, he never growled at me. By the same token, if he had an 'accident' on the floor, I'd clean it up and never scold him.

When he chewed up my favorite baseball hat, I bought another and never scolded him. Nino was good with people who approached me, never growling, or nipping at them.

Having said that, heaven forbid anyone to ever raise their voice to me; or worse yet act as if they were to attack me. Nino made it plain, on more than one occasion, that he would not tolerate any hostile moves on his master.

In each case, and there were only two I can recall, a hefty growl and the showing sharp canines convinced the 'scooter-bags' it was in their best interest to cease and stop.

After several years with the 122 Precinct, I got transferred to Manhattan.

Unfortunately, I had to move closer to the station. In so doing I went from a home in the countryside to an apartment in the city. The apartment owners' would not allow pets, so I ask a friend of mine to take Nino. It broke my heart to give him up, but I knew I'd still be able to see him.

Every chance I got I'd stop in and see Nino. He'd see me coming and he'd go into a frenzy, jumping about and wagging his tail. I'd pet and hug him as he licked my face. We'd share precious moments and then I'd have to leave. Nino would watch me go, and if he'd had tear glands his eyes would have overflowed; mine did.

One day, about two years after I'd let my friend take Nino, I went to see him. When I pulled into the drive, I looked to where Nino usually stayed, near the garage. I didn't see Nino, so I walked to the garage and then to its rear: No Nino. My friend, seeing me out his kitchen window, came out.

"Hey Al, where's Nino?" I asked.

"He nipped at my son, so I shot him," Al said, coldly.

"You what!"

"I shot him. He bit my son."

Al pointed out where Nino was laying.

Al's son, Johnny, was about three years old at the time.

"Nino would never bite your son," I said, my voice breaking. My eyes filled with tears, and I felt my face flush. I took Nino to a nearby animal hospital. The doctor informed me that Nino will recover.

Let me tell you what happened with Al…

"Well, he bit Johnny. I wanted to get rid of him," Al said, as if he'd just crushed a bug.

I couldn't believe what I was hearing: My Nino, was almost killed by this monster….

"Why didn't you call me? You didn't have to shoot him!"

I thought back to when Al and I had worked together. I recalled once when he and another cop had found an injured dog on the side of the street. A citizen had called them about the animal.

Al and his partner had taken the animal to a secluded wooded area and shot it. I thought, when I'd heard what they'd done, that it wasn't right but maybe they'd just wanted to put the dog out of its misery. Maybe I was wrong, I thought. Maybe Al enjoyed doing that stuff.

I was devastated. I was so mad I couldn't stay near where Al stood. I left without saying another word.

Since I had over 25 years on the force, I could have full retirement benefits. I'm retired now. I still have my Nino.

I got myself a small cottage for Nino and me….

Chapter 6

The Arrest

An echoed across the sleeping street as a man in black suit and a hat which had been carelessly left on the street.

The shadow stumbled up quickly and put the lid back where he found it. He continued his way to the big mansion across the street.

As soon as he arrived at the door, he unscrewed the silver knocker and carefully and quietly cut a hole in the glass near the doorknob.

He stuck his hand through an unlocked door. The man in black opened the door and looked around the huge entrance hall. He was Roy and he had a life of crime. He started at the age of 8 with shoplifting.

When he turned 19, he graduated to street fights and drinks. At 23 he started robbing houses and cars.

Now, almost 40, he was ready for more risky crimes. This was one of them; this house had so many people living in it that even the slightest noise could get him in big trouble.

Looking around he saw a few things that caught his attention. After raiding the house and having several close calls he made his way home. As he was leaving, something caught his eye; a Red Lamborghini Diablo…

Driving home in his newly acquired Lamborghini, loaded with loot, Roy decided to show his wife the things he had stolen.

At home his wife was watching TV. Quietly Roy took a beer from the fridge and threw it at the TV. SMASH! The glass shattered into millions of tiny pieces. "You're home dear?" said Roy's wife without even balking at the broken glass.

"So did you get anything nice?" She asked. "Of course, what do you think?" said Roy as he picked up the broken TV and replaced it with the new Plasma TV that he had just stolen.

After showing his wife the rest of his loot, he remembered that his birthday was the following day. "I'm ready." He said, "Ready for what dear?" asked his wife "I'm ready to rob in the daylight."

Parking his new car just around the corner, Roy was ready for action. He was just about to pick up the lock when he heard sirens.

"Oh damn!" he shouted as he rushed back to his stolen car. He drove away as quickly as possible only to find that he was being chased by three Police cars!

Going as fast as he could he eventually thought he had lost them, but the next minute he was surrounded by Police Officers.

He angrily stepped on the gas, going straight into the Police car in front of him. SMASH! As soon as the rest of the force saw the car fly, they wrestled Roy out of his car and onto the ground arresting him! Roy's days of crime ended in broad daylight!!

Chapter 7

Walking the Beat

The police officer moved along the street, strong and important. This was the way he always moved. He was not thinking of how he looked. There were few people on the street to see him. It was only about ten at night, but it was cold.

There was a wind with a little rain in it. He stopped at doors as he walked along, He was trying each door to be sure that it was closed for the night.

Now and then he turned and looked up and down the street. He was a fine-looking cop, watchful, guarding the peace. People in this part of the city went home early. Now and then you might see the lights of a shop or of a small restaurant. But most of the doors belonged to business places that had been closed hours ago.

Then the cop suddenly slowed his walk. Near the door of a darkened shop a man was standing. As the cop walked toward him, the man spoke quickly.

"It's all right, officer," he said. "I'm waiting for a friend. Twenty years ago, we agreed to meet here tonight. It sounds strange to you, doesn't it? I'll explain if you want to be sure that everything's all right.

About twenty years ago there was a restaurant where this shop stands.

"Joe's Restaurant." "It was here until five years ago," said the cop.

The man near the door had a colorless square face with bright eyes, and a little white mark near his right eye. He had a large jewel in his necktie.

"Twenty years ago, tonight," said the man, "I had dinner here with Jimmy Suarez. He was my best friend and the best fellow in the world.

He and I grew up together here in New York, like two brothers. I was eighteen and Jimmy was twenty. The next morning, I was to start for the

West. I was going to find a job and make a great success. You couldn't have pulled Jimmy out of New York. He thought it was the only place.

"We agreed that night that we would meet here again in twenty years. We thought that in twenty years we would know what kind of men we were, and what future waited for us."

"It sounds interesting," said the cop. "A long time between meetings, it seems to me. Have you heard from your friend since you went West?"

"Yes, for a time we did write to each other," said the man. "After a year or two, we stopped. The West is big. I moved around everywhere, and I moved quickly. I know that Jimmy will meet me here if he can. He was as true as any man in the world. He'll never forget.

I came a thousand miles to stand here tonight. I'll be glad about. that, if my old friend comes too."

The waiting man took out a fine watch, covered with small jewels.

"Three minutes before ten," he said. "It was ten that night when. We said goodbye here at the restaurant door."

"You were successful in the West, weren't you?" asked the cop.

"I surely was! I hope Jimmy has done half as well. He was a slow mover. I've had to fight for my success.

In New York a man doesn't change much. In the West you learn how to fight for what you get."....

The cop took a step or two. "I'll go on my way," he said. "I hope your friend comes all right. If he isn't here at ten, are you going to leave?"

"I am not!" said the other. "I'll wait half an hour, at least. If Jimmy is alive on earth, he'll be here by that time. Good night, officer."

"Good night," said the cop, and walked away, trying doors as he went.

There was now a cold rain falling and the wind was stronger. The few people walking along that street were hurrying, trying to keep warm.

At the door of the shop, stood the man who had come a thousand miles to meet a friend. Such a meeting could not be certain, however, he waited.

About twenty minutes he waited, and then a tall man in a long coat came hurrying across the street. He went directly to the waiting. man.

"Is that you, Bob?" he asked, doubtfully.

"Is that you, Jimmy ?" cried the man at the door.

The new man took the other man's hands in his. "It's Bob! It surely is. I was certain I would find you here if you were still alive. Twenty years is a long time. The old restaurant is gone, Bob. I wish it were here, so that we could have another dinner in it. Has the West been good to you?"

"It gave me everything I asked for. You've changed, Jimmy. I never thought you were so tall."

"Oh, I grew a little after I was twenty.

"Are you doing well in New York, Jimmy?"

"Well, enough. I work for the city. Come on, Bob, we'll go to a place I know and have a good long talk about old times."

The two men started along the street, arm in arm. The man from the West was beginning to tell the story of his life.

Bob and Jimmy were friends when they were young, and now they will grow old together....

Chapter 8

The Suspect

When the police forcibly entered 43-year-old Paulina Fiore's apartment, they found her lifeless body on the floor of the kitchen, covered in mysterious bruises. The lead detective immediately suspected homicide and ordered an autopsy. But after extensive analysis, the coroner concluded the cause of death was vitamin C deficiency.

In a video appearing on social media, Stephanie Brolo, who sources confirm is a close friend of Paulina, is seen weeping and uttering, "This is all my fault."

At the offices of my city's largest newspaper, I sip my third espresso of the morning and finish writing the story. One coffee per story is a good rule to live by. I wish I could teach this to new journalists, but they have their own ways of doing things.

After I finish my third random fatality writeup of the morning, I announce "I'm sick of tabloid journalism!" to the newsroom to no one in particular. The young writers around me ignore me. In the economic downturn in traditional media, they are happy to simply hold a job.

Giuseppe, our new Chief Editor, says articles with a topic of either sex or death receive ten times more clicks than any other. The editorial concepts in his head are as blunt as the sales method of a fish seller in the market. I need to endure another month of ambulance chasing until I can focus on another piece of investigative journalism.

My lengthy expose of government corruption last month, which filled half the front page of the print edition, received fewer views online than a weekend car crash or a nightclub brawl.

"Mike?" Giuseppe is standing in front of my desk. "Why haven't you interviewed the friend yet?"

"Friend? Friend of whom?"

"Idiot. The 'It's all my fault' friend. Young, attractive, trending online?" Giuseppe says this with his voice rising in volume for each word.

"Stephanie Bustelo." I show Giuseppe my memory for detail is flawless. "I didn't study Political Science to chase after friends of murder victims and suicides."

"Do it." He turns around and stomps off. Halfway across the newsroom, he turns back and shouts, "Vitamin C! Focus on the vitamin C. Nutrition stories are good for our advertisers, Max."

Several reporters type notes into their mobiles. Even an untrained eye can foresee them proposing all types of vitamin stories in tomorrow's news meeting.

I dial the friend.

"This is Mike Sewall. Is this Bianca?"

"Yes," a female voice says, and hesitates. "Are you with the police?"

"No. I'm with the…" I say the name of the newspaper. With a 137-year history, the name often opens doors.

"I thought the police would be the first to call. What do you want?"

The police in Italy would never bother with something as trivial as a comment on social media. Unless a politician or celebrity was involved.

"I'd like to clarify what you said in the viral video on ItaliaApp." I mention Italy's largest social media app.

"That video is ruining my life," Bianca says.

"I'm sorry to hear that."

"Well, everyone misunderstood what I said. I didn't have anything to do with Paulina's death. She stopped going out and looked thinner six months ago. Maybe I started her in this direction…", she catches her breath. "I only called her twice after she stopped seeing me. I should have tried harder, gone to her home…"

"Yes?"

"It's all too much," she says, "Thanks for calling me, but sorry, I don't know who you are."

Abruptly, the mobile screen turns red. She disconnects the WhatsApp call and goes offline.

"Good work on the Paulina interview." Giuseppe reaches over and picks up one of my antique pencils and massages it between his fingers.

"No problem, boss." I managed to knit the meager information I was given into a piece about a heartbroken friend and a substantial essay about eating disorders.

"Nice pencil." He studies the Castelli wooden pencil quixotically. "Mike, you are ten years too old for this newsroom. You are a cat that always lands on its feet."

"The Tiger of Turin?" I propose. "I'll accept that as a byline."

An important sounding moniker is the best I can hope for these days. I recall the Elysian Days of being flown to Rome to interview government ministers, back when traditional newspapers collected all the advertising revenue instead of Google.

When assigned a story, one of the first duties a beat reporter checks off is to contact the family members. I locate Paulina's father on social media and send an introduction:

This is Max Sewall, a reporter with the Metro Register. I'm writing an article about the unfortunate incident with your daughter and would like to ensure I have all details correct. Please contact me at your earliest convenience.

I receive a reply, which appears to be copied & pasted:

"We have nothing to say, do not contact us again. "The Fiore Family"

I move on to another breaking story, and the Paulina story goes quiet in the newsroom of the Metro Register for several days.

"Max. Line 7!" someone shouts.

I answer, "City desk, Mike Sewall."

"This is Paulina Fiore's father," a man says, "our daughter. It's all our fault. We saw how much time she was spending on her mobile and never stopped her."

"I'm sure it's not your fault, but I would like to hear more," I say, "Is there a reason you decided to call me today?"

"The police unlocked her phone and asked us questions about the websites she was looking at."

"Do you remember any of the names?"

"I don't know. I've never heard of any of them," he said, "But most of the articles were about diseases."

"Was she in contact with anyone?"

"They did say she received the links from friends on the Italian."

Judging by reports from neighbors, Paulina has not been outside for months. The friends must be online ones.

I call Professor Rizzo at the University of Toranto.

"Could fear about disease, viruses and bacteria and so on, cause a patient to suffer from malnutrition?" I ask.

"Mysophobia, commonly called germaphobia, can cause a patient to avoid touching food, to eat with gloves, that sort of thing. In problem cases, it may cause patients to limit social interaction and avoid public places."

"Paulina appeared to be living on a diet of boiled pasta."

"That sounds possible, but I've never heard of malnutrition even in the most extreme cases of Mysophobia. Hunger, including a desire for a mixed diet, is stronger than almost any other psychological urge."

"But isn't the urge to survive even stronger?" I conjecture, trying to imagine what the existential threat could be.

How could Paulina completely avoid something so widespread as vitamin C? I update the Chief Editor on my progress on the case.

"This has the workings of a good human interest story, food, fear, a female victim." Giuseppe looks satisfied. "Keep digging but steer clear from anything negative about Italia App. They deliver 30% of our incoming traffic."

I am on speaking terms with many people in our city. People love to talk about themselves to someone who is actively listening. Especially if they perceive them to be in a position of authority.

After graduating university together, Bruno went on a different, more international path than I. Having worked for 15 years in Silicon Valley, he returned to our hometown and was soon snapped up by Italy's largest social media company. A glimpse at a life I could have lived.

I cancel dinner with my girlfriend Gabrielle to set up a cozy dinner with a 41-year-old man.

On a clear dry evening as dusk descends over T as it sits in its valley between the towering Italian Alps on one side and the rolling hills that rise up from the River on the other, I walk toward the rectangular bulk of iron lattice that is the old Fiat factory in Lingotto on the south side of the city.

The factory, almost a kilometer long, has transformed into offices and a ground floor shopping mall. Now it's popular with high-tech startups, many from America, France, and Germany.

The building that was the epicenter of the city when Turin produced half the automobile of Europe is now filled with people trying to figure out how to sell discount handbags through ecommerce. At least the people of Turin are no longer destined for a life of hard labor as previous generations were.

Paulina lived not far from this building.

At the Osteria del Fiat I've asked for a quiet table. I'm disappointed when the host leads us to a very crowded dining room. We pass a large room with only one table of guests.

In the circle of suited men, I recognize a retired local politician. In the dark recesses of the city, the power brokers don't like to be overheard.

An hour later after we finished our own dinner, Bruno takes a large drink of the Dolcetto d'Alba we have been drinking. The obligatory pleasantries and the exchange of information about shared friends has been completed and we can move on to the real meat of the dinner.

I will explain how Paulina had been accessing his employer's App over 50 times a day.

"At Italia App we focus on returning traffic. Some readers we enchant with glamour, others we addict with fear."

"Isn't that manipulation?"

"We are giving people what they want. If they want to hate, they will find it. If they want to love, they will find that too."

"What about promoting democracy and humanitarian values?"

"That's just rhetoric for university students. You know that."

"Paulina Fiore died after reading on fake news sent to her by ItaliaApp."

"It's not our fault it someone can't handle online news. If we don't send it to them, someone else will."

"You have become very American in your thinking," I point out. It's disappointing my old friend can't see the world the same way we used to, but I've become resigned to accept people's differences, politically or otherwise. "The police seem very interested in her social media history," I add.

Bruno looks at me with renewed interest, "Have the police opened an investigation?"

"Maybe her death is not ItaliaApp's fault, maybe it's the people who write the fake news. If you can send me her browsing history, the one the police are going through, I'll look and put some spotlight **on the** fake new producers. That might keep you one step ahead in reacting to negative coverage. I'll keep your name out of it, of course."

"I'll think about it." Bruno focuses on his red wine glass.

Bruno and I may not see eye to eye, but we have enough shared history to trust we will protect each other's best interests. The next afternoon, I received Paulina's browsing history via an encrypted messaging app.

I start clicking through the links:

Italy's continuing flood of illegal immigrants.

How Covid rises through ventilation shafts.

The 7 Ways Elevator buttons spread Disease.

Paparazzi capture pictures of Italy's first Monkeypox patient.

Vegetables in our Supermarkets picked by Immigrants Inundated with Monkey Pox Virus.

I scan through months of links about deadly diseases and ways to avoid them. Fake news is a problem, and the government has been trying to combat it.

In the thousands of links, I scan through, my heart flutters as I spot our name.

"Don't trust what the government says about Monkey Pox. See attached articles from the Metro Register."

Clicking the link, I see a list of familiar headlines:

The Dark Hand Behind the Government Reshuffle - Max Serafino

Patient Malpractice Allegations Covered up by Health Authorities - Max Serafino

Pandemic Recommendations Misguided – Mike Sewall

Corruption Exposed in Turin Government - Mike Sewall

Other articles Paulina was reading, those not to trust doctors and government health advice, often link to articles written by me and my colleagues.

I stare at the pencil that sits on my desk where Giuseppe left it earlier. Behind me, I hear someone approach, and feel their hands on my shoulders.

Giuseppe's voice says, "And you thought you were superior to all of us, didn't you?"

"Is it all...?" I am about to ask an obvious question. Stop me. I have bills to pay and a scarcity of other work alternatives. I sweep pointless self-doubt from my mind. Journalists report the news, we do not generate it.

With a click of the mouse, I bring up today's police bulletin, and make proposals on which events we might cover for our prestigious 137-year-old newspaper to the Chief Editor.

The next morning, a young journalist who normally sits beside me walks triumphantly through the newsroom greeting colleagues. Giuseppe gives him a thumbs up. I open the Metro Register's most viewed list, an online article, "Clickbait News Causes Scurvy in Italy's Auto Capital" is trending across the nation.

I begin having regular dinners with Bruno. We talk about our old adventures in school, and about the state of the country, Bruno reminds me that a Political Science professor in university had taught us, "Every industry is selling a product, and at its core, the news industry sells fear."

In the coming months the number of cases of malnutrition like Paulina's snowball across the nation. I notice Bruno starts to eat more and more. I have lost my appetite.

Chapter 9

The Soldier

The air hung heavy with the foggy dew of a February morning.

Through the single-pane window, dampened though it was, could be heard the regimented tramp of a platoon of British Lancers. The melodic jingle of them was harmonized by the footfall of their heavy boots. They passed by unseen in the fog.

The well-worn sound of sirens echoed down the street as they had done from early morning but neither of us paid heed. Nothing new for a Belfast morning.

I sat rigid at the table, uncomfortable in the starched school shirt that was too small but 'would see me through to the end of the year', whilst Ma poured the cornflakes into the bowl before me. The tinkle of them played merrily against the threatening chorus outside.

A little milk splashed free onto the table as she filled the bowl, seeping its way down the tables grains before a cloth could had.

"Hurry yourself up or you'll be late," Ma said before dragging the hairbrush through my tattered mane, the futility of it lost on her - though her annoyance was clear when I ran my fingers through it, immediately undoing her hard work.

From the counter, the little radio spat and crackled out a song my mother liked, and she hummed to herself as she flitted from mother-job to mother-job; cleaning and wiping, hanging the wet clothes, folding the dry.

I shoveled in a mouthful. The crunch drowns out the world around me.

"Ma, sugar please," I said, mouth still full, sending a burst cornflake shrapnel into the air.

She whisked the sugar over to me and wiped down the table once more, humming out the dying notes of the song.

Dad's absence wasn't even registered by Ma and I. He was never there in the mornings.

He was the milkman, passing through the local streets in his van before the cocks had time to clear their throats, swapping empty bottles for full ones, often with only the dawning sun for company.

He'd tut and he'd sigh as he trundled past the burnt-out cars and the bombed-out bars of Belfast. He'd nod to soldier and gunman alike as he made his rounds for few others were out on the streets that early.

That's how he was; open, friendly, peaceful.

"We're all born the same, we all die the same," he'd say, "and we're all the same in between."

That's how he raised me, free from hatred and division.

I took another mouthful, much more to my taste this time, the flakes not offering as much resistance.

"Fix your tie, will you? You look like you were reared in a field, that's no way to be heading off to school."

The usual scolding from Ma on a school morning.

The song ended and the radio rang out eight bells. A familiar voice greeted us.

"Good morning, the headlines."

We continued our customs, me chewing, Ma cleaning.

Crunch, wipe, fold.

And the radio said, "There's another shot dead on the streets of Belfast. Early reports say he died with a gun in his hand."

Crunch, wipe, fold.

The reporter prattled on, other disturbances, the humdrum of the politicians, the rise of fuel costs. Another Belfast morning, the same old routine.

Crunch, wipe, fold.

It was the knock at the door, the three heavy raps, that broke the dullness.

I looked at Ma, her eyes as wide as my own.

With Da on the rounds, I was the man of the house. I started to rise, but Ma's firm hand returned me to my seat.

"Stay," she ordered, and I obeyed.

I watched her as she stepped from the kitchen, drying cloth in hand.

I heard her gasp from the hallway as she opened the door. I knew what that meant.

The chill of the foggy dew that rushed through the open door seized me.

The officer stood the entire time, directly across from me in the kitchen. Between us, upon the table, the bowl lay unfinished; islands of orange flakes bobbing on a placid sea of white.

The radio was silent now, freeing the stage for the solemn tick-tock of the clock.

He stood there. His uniform was clean and crisp with the dark green jacket buttoned professionally. He did not remove his cap, emblazoned with a harp donning a crown.

"I'm very sorry," he said without emotion, "very sorry for your loss."

He cleared his throat and looked between Ma and I. She was still crying, but it was silent now. Her reddened eyes bore the pain which was spilling over blotched cheeks.

I was numb.

I stared at his tie. It was fitted right up to the collar, neat to his neck. He wasn't reared in a field I thought.

"How-" Ma started but was ambushed by a sob.

The officer cleared his throat again.

"He was seen walking up Fitzgibbons Street with what I'm told, was a revolver. The army opened fire and he... well, he..."

The officer blinked hard and cleared his throat again.

"I'm very sorry," he repeated.

The silence that feels rotted into an intolerable discomfort, putrefying the air. Another throat clear did nothing to shift it.

"No," I said though my throat was dry, "Da wouldn't have- he couldn't have- he didn't have a gun. He wasn't involved."

The officer nodded to pacify me, but his eyes betrayed his lack of belief.

"We will, of course, carry out a full investigation once the army have completed their assessment."

Empty words I thought.

The officer saw himself out and in his wake was left the true absence of Dad.

In the bowl, the cornflakes were sudden.

It took twelve years. Twelve tormenting years and an independent commission for the truth to come to light.

Call it what you want. There was no gun.

The soldier had mistaken a bottle of milk for a revolver and had opened fire without a word of warning.

My Dad. Dead. Over a bottle of milk.

They say there's no point crying over spilt milk. I hate that saying.

Ma never got over it, went to her grave without the truth and now lies beside Dad, just like they did in their bed. Born the same. Died the same.

I enlisted as soon as I could. Not to free my country, not for injustice. Just for revenge.

I have done awful things. Terrible things.

But I make no moans about it. I do not apologize for it, to any man or God.

We are born the same. We die the same. But we are not the same.

I am not the same as I was. I changed at eight o'clock that February morning.

So now here I lie, in the foggy dew of the morning, with my rifle, awaiting the jingle of an oncoming platoon.

I wonder what the radio will say.

Chapter 10

The Missing Husband

Helen and her young neighbor slid the oak tree into a deep hole dug in the soil.

"Hold it straight, now," Helen says gruffly as she shovels dirt around the root ball.

"I can do this part if you want. I'm younger and, uh," the neighbor trails off as Hestia gives her best scathing look.

They finish the task in silence.

Around 20 Hours earlier....

Helen opens another Diet Coke, the crack and fizzle a welcome sound to her ears. She knows it will be the death of her, but it is her choice, and she will gladly take it to the grave.

When the acidic bite of the first sip fades, she raises the binoculars with one twisted old hand and peers Westward between the cracked blinds of her bedroom window.

It is a good window, an upper story window that faces her back yard and more importantly, her neighbors back yards. She pays a neighborhood boy to haul his 10-foot ladder over and clean it from the outside once a week.

Nearly a year ago, while on a walk with her dog, Peanut, she had seen him cleaning out gutters. Now, she gives him 2 dollars a week for the single window. The others she can do for herself, as they are all on the first floor.

Once, he'd tried to dicker with her, but she'd whopped him on the back of the head and told him to respect his elders. He'd glared at her then but nodded, and the deal was struck.

She needs the binoculars to see the house two down from her, number 17. A family lives there, a nice one if you didn't know any better; a couple, two small children with angelic blonde hair, and a big dumb dog. As it is, the dog likes to chase poor Peanut and the kids cause an awful ruckus when they play out back.

Plus, children are not interesting. She'd written them a very pointed letter where she suggested a shorter outside play time and a shorter leash for their menacing mutt. Yet, the Heathens ignored her letter, and the snot-nosed brats continue to do whatever they please, to Hell with everyone else. The new generation is doomed, she is sure of it.

Hestia had then spent several satisfying weeks tipping over their trashcan until she noticed that the tell-tale red light of a security camera had appeared on their front porch, and now she is forced to consider alternative methods of punishment. Currently, their yard is empty, and their windows are dark.

She belches loudly and turns to yell for Peanut, who either can't hear her or ignores her. He is getting old, 14 or 15, so she can't tell if he is hard of hearing or is being purposely disrespectful. She narrows her eyes, mutters, and turns back to the window.

The house sandwiched between the Heathens house and her own, number 18, is quite boring. An old man lives there. He is older than her, single, and he has no discernible family or friends. No one ever visits, and rarely does he leave. His groceries are delivered to his front porch once a week– very new age of him. His name is Arthur, but she calls him Humpy because he looks like an egg.

Humpy likes gardening, and more than once she'd had a go at him for letting his rose bushes creep between the cracks of the fence that separated their properties. Honestly, she doesn't care much about it but wants to see him riled up. He is, unfortunately, unflappable. She spends the least amount of time watching Humpty and hopes he will die soon so that someone else will move in.

She takes another gulp of Diet Coke and calls Peanut again. This time, the elderly chihuahua pads into the room and lays down on the threadbare dog bed near her feet. She croons to him softly and nudges the bowl of Old Roy's towards him which he sniffs, unimpressed, and lays his head down. Hestia rolls her neck several times, finishes her drink, and tosses it in a white trashcan overflowing with identical cans.

She peers out the window in her own back yard. It is overgrown and unkempt. Her husband, may he rot in Hell, had been crazy about the lawn. He'd worn spiked shoes when walking on it, lest he leave any footprints, and he forbade her from ever stepping foot on it.

He would often go out just to prune a single branch and then come back inside and stare out into the back yard as if willing everything to grow just so. After he died, she'd taken great pleasure in watching the yard become wild and unruly. The dickering window boy had offered his services for that as well, which she'd declined acidly.

She lifts the binoculars and peers Easterly to the house two doors down in the other direction, number 21. It is a vacant house which has been on the market for eight months. Hestia concludes that the woman who is selling it mustn't be desperate for money since she has been too stubborn to lower the outrageous asking price.

So, the place has fallen into disrepair during its lengthy inoccupancy. The yard is cut once a month by persons unknown, but as it is summer, it often looks as wild as her own.

Finally, she turns to her most interesting neighbors, number 20. A young couple moved in a year ago and things were quiet at first. She guessed they were 30 or 35 years old. The woman has bright red hair and likes to read on the back porch when the sun is low in the sky.

The man has a dark complexion and looks foreign -- Serbian? Columbian? -- she doesn't know, all foreigners look the same to her. She calls them Jack and Diane. Diane occasionally waves at her from the front porch when their comings and goings coincide. Hestia appreciates the neighborliness and decides, magnanimously, not to send them a letter about parking their car so cattywampus.

They don't play loud music and they don't have kids or dogs. The man keeps the lawn short and the bushes meticulously trimmed and shaped. But no one knows better than the darkness that hides behind the costume of a carefully manicured lawn.

Eventually, the fights began; huge blow outs that spilled through the screen door where she can clearly hear them when she cracks her window. The general flow of these goes like this: Diane, who seems generally quiet and reserved, will argue whatever point she is trying to make.

Then, Jack will inevitably start yelling over her, and Diane will take it for a while until eventually her composure is lost and she starts screaming in this high-pitched psychotic tone where Hestia can barely understand what she is saying.

Sometimes, there is the sound of breaking glass or slamming doors. Occasionally, the sound of a car door, an engine revving, and a car speeding away from the house. Those are becoming more common place, so Hestia greedily watches number 20 whenever she can. Hestia hopes Diane gives as good as she gets. There had been a particularly nasty argument about money earlier, but all is quiet now.

When nothing happens for several long minutes, Hestia sighs and resigns herself to another lonesome night watching CSI with Peanut. She makes her way downstairs to the kitchen and retrieves a frozen dinner from the icebox and heats it up. She settles into the dingy couch in her living room and watches reruns while she finishes her dinner and promptly falls asleep as the sun retreats beneath the horizon.

She dreams that her dead husband is alive and standing at the foot of her bed holding his beloved hedge trimmers, a dark substance dripping off their sharpened tips. She wakes up sometime later startled and disoriented. Peanut is snoring lightly beside her, his tongue hanging out the side of his mouth where several of his teeth are missing.

She listens intently, but the only other sound is the quiet tick tick tick of the kitchen clock. She can't fathom what time it is, but it seems preternaturally dark. She groans from standing and makes her way up the stairs to her bedroom. She peers outside and sees that the moon is barely a sliver in the sky.

A glance at the bright red numbers on her bedside clock tells her that it is 2:59 AM. Her neck is stiff, and she gingerly turns her head this way and that to try to ease the ache she knows will still be there in the morning.

She jumps, still on edge from her nightmare. She brings one hand to her racing heart and wishes it to slow.

She edges towards the window and waits for her eyes to adjust to the nearly moonless night.

There. She sees the vague outline of a hooded figure in the yard at number 20. They are near the edge of the property line where carefully tended grass meets suburban woods. What are they doing? Is it Jack or Diane? It is impossible to tell.

Hestia's hand flew to her mouth in sudden realization. Her eyes are fully adjusted to the scant light now and she can see that they are digging, the metallic glint of the shovel appearing and disappearing beneath the earth with each successive clink.

Now, why would someone be digging a hole at this hour? There is only one reason she can think of, and it isn't to get a leg up on the gardening before the summer heat rolls in.

She knows it instinctively, not just because of the couple's explosive fights, but also because she herself has thought about doing the same thing to her husband a million times before the scoundrel had the gall to drop dead of his own accord.

The real question is which one of them is doing the digging?

Hestia watches, transfixed, as the person continues to dig. An hour pass, then two, then three. She nods off in her chair twice only to snap awake moments later, unable to stop watching the crime unfold. It takes much longer to dig a grave than I thought, she thinks. And then, what a stupid place to bury someone.

Just before dawn, the figure walks back towards the house and disappears for several long minutes. When they return, they are dragging a misshapen bundle slowly towards the too-shallow pit. When the figure reaches the grave, the hood of their jacket slips back revealing red hair so vivid that it is impossible to miss even in the darkness. Not realizing she has been holding her breath, Hestia lets out a gasp of delight.

"You naughty girl," she says, a Cheshire grin spreading across her face. It is unfamiliar, the smile, and she realizes it is the first one in a long while. She lets her mind wander into a daydream where she is the one doing the digging.

The grin slides off her face, however, when she realizes that Diane is sure to get caught. One didn't report a person missing and got away with a fresh mound of dirt in the back yard, did they?

But perhaps Diane wouldn't report her husband missing. No, she quickly casts that idea aside. Hestia knows that Jack's mother stops by regularly, she drives a horrible little minivan that backfires obscene, and she occasionally joins her son in casting noisy aspersions at poor Diane.

The woman would unquestionably look for her son, no doubt about it. Diane's goose is as good as cooked.

Unless…

The rusty wheels in Hestia's mind turn more quickly now. Unless someone else intervened.

By 3 PM the next day, Hestia's yard is looking more like it did in its previous life. The hedges are trimmed, the grass is cut and watered, flowering shrubs are planted, and one dickering neighbor boy is $100 richer. Hestia complains aloud to Peanut but is secretly quite satisfied at her progress. Like clockwork,

Diane's car rolls into the short driveway of number 20 at 3:45 PM. This pleases Hestia, who had been worried that Diane may have done a runner when her car pulled out of her driveway at 7 am. Based on the time, Hestia concludes that she must have gone to work to keep up appearances. Smart girl.

Now that she is certain that Diane will be around to appreciate her thoughtful plan, she collects her notebook and makes a draft of what she will say to the police.

That night, Hestia creeps into the silent backyard of Number 20 and digs up Jack's poorly concealed body and drags it back to her own. She rolls it into the deep hole she had the neighbor boy dig and covers it with a layer of dirt and then a layer of manure, leaving a foot of unfilled space which she will address the following morning.

The redhead hands her strange old neighbor her spare suitcase. "Here. Where did you say you were going again?"

"Florida. Airport broke my old luggage," Hestia says, waving a hand.

"And now you want me to help you plant a tree?" Diane asks slowly, trying to understand. She has never spoken more than a quick greeting to her neighbor in the entire year that she's lived next door.

Hestia thinks Diane looks like Hell has swallowed her and spat her back out. She has cut lips, and a black eye and Hestia speculates if she went to work after all. The redhead's eyes are dull, and her clothes are a wrinkled mess. Hestia has no doubt that if Diane was her usual self, she would be more suspicious.

"I'm an old woman," Hestia says by way of explanation. She is, in fact, quite sore from the previous night's activities.

"Er, I'm a little busy," Diane says.

"It'll only take a minute. I just need someone to hold the tree steady."

"Okay," Diane says reluctantly.

Minutes later, Hestia and her young neighbor slide the oak sapling into the gaping hole dug in the earth.

"Hold it straight, now," Hestia says gruffly as she shovels dirt around the root ball.

"I can do this part if you want. I'm younger and, uh," the neighbor trails off as Hestia gives her best scathing look.

They finish the task in silence.

When they return to the front yard and Diane turns towards her house, Hestia quickly offers to make some fresh lemonade, well, the powdered kind, anyway, to thank her for her help. Diane shrugs noncommittally.

"Great!" Hestia says a little too loudly and quickly makes her way to her kitchen, stashes the luggage in the hall closet, and promptly phones the police. She makes the lemonade slowly and comes outside just as two police cruisers park in front of Number 20.

Balancing the tray with lemonade and a stack of plastic cups, she shuffles over to Diane, who looks like she is going to be sick as the police officers exit their vehicles.

Hestia leans closer to her neighbor, imagining that she is in one of her favorite crime dramas.

"Listen to me. Get a lawyer, say nothing. Follow my lead," she mutters under her breath, barely moving her lips.

Despite her apparent terror, Diane turns to look at her shrewdly, her eyes narrowed into slits.

"Good morning officers," Hestia says brightly, wondering if she sounds as fake to their ears as she does her own. "Would you like some lemonade?"

"Ma'am. Miss," one of the officers says, nodding his head. "No thank you, we're here on official business." He turns towards Diane. "Do you live at this residence? Number 20?"

Diane nods, not trusting herself to speak.

The second officer turns to Hestia and says, "Ma'am, this is a private matter. I'll ask that you return home now, please." Ah, so you're the Bad Cop, then.

"Well, you see, I'm the one who phoned you, actually," Hestia says sheepishly.

Diane looks at her, one eye wide, one eye swollen half shut.

"Is that so…?" Bad Cop sends Good Cop a conspicuous look. "We'll talk to you both separately, then. Ma'am, would you kindly lead me to your place of residence?" Hestia catches Diane's gaze one final time makes a subtle zipper motion over her lips and allows the officers to lead them in separate directions.

This isn't exactly the way she had planned for things to go. She thought she'd make a big stink of things in front of Diane, explaining that Jack was abusive, and Hestia couldn't take the fights and didn't want poor Diane to get hurt anymore. That Jack had run off on foot and she had seen him with a suitcase walking that way in the direction of the bus station.

Now they are separated and there is no time to get their stories straight. Hestia bites her lip hard enough to draw blood and hopes that Diane doesn't incriminate herself or all of Hestia's careful planning will be for naught.

At the end, something Diane says or does is suspicious enough that she is labeled a person of interest and carted off to the police station. Later, more officers appear and search the premises of Number 20 where they find blood, but it is almost all Diane's.

They also find the freshly mixed dirt in the back yard and a team is sent with an excavator to dig it up, where they turn up nothing but worms. After two days, the authorities are forced to release her due to insufficient evidence, much to her confusion.

In time, the tiny sapling in Hestia's backyard grows into a beautiful Oak tree and no one is the wiser, not even Diane, as to what lay beneath.

Chapter 11

Junior is Missing

Grandma is dying but she has lived a long and good life. At the age of ninety-seven, she was in remarkably good shape until a cancer diagnosis three months ago.

She made it clear from the start that she didn't want to fight it. No chemo, no radiation, no surgeries. "Just keep me comfortable and let me die in my own home," was all she asked.

My sister, Laurie, and I were supposed to be taking turns staying with her in her house, but Laurie works a lot. I am basically staying here full-time. Fortunately, my job is a remote research position.

Grandma was skeptical when I told her that I could work from home, or from her house or wherever I happened to be. For her a job is a place to go every day, not something you can do just by opening your laptop.

I set up a makeshift office at her dining room table. After working in silence for a few hours, I decided to check on grandma. Sure enough, she is asleep in her room. I have noticed that she is sleeping more and has more episodes of confusion.

Hospice comes by once a day to check her vitals, see if she needs more meds and let us know how she is doing.

I begin to think about my grandma's life. Life that is about to end. I need to think about that, about the obituary anyway. I begin making some notes.

'Born Annie Lee Morton in 1928, to Deborah and LeRoy Morton, she grew up in Smith County. At the age of sixteen, she got a job at the snack counter of the old Songbird Drugstore. It was there she met John Joseph Lane or JoJo as everyone called him. They married in 1950 and welcomed a son in 1955.

Mrs. Lane went on to move to Livingston. She began a job with the Renault Insurance Agency as a secretary in 1964, where she worked until her retirement in 2002. In her retirement, Mrs. Lane remained active with the local theater, as a library volunteer and with local charities.

Many in the community remember her warmly. She was preceded in death by her son, Jacob Lane, several years ago. She is survived by his daughters, Laurie, and Maddie Lane.'

I stare at the notes in front of me. I can't believe that is all there is, after 97 years. There should be more.

I look out the window. The backyard is filled with dry brown leaves. My grandmother always kept everything so tidy, and the yard was no exception. Until the cancer, she raked those leaves herself. "If she looks out her bedroom window, she will see how neglected the yard is," I think.

I retrieve the rake from the backyard shed and I think about the short obituary. The truth is that grandma's life had one big black hole. It was the void left by her husband and my grandfather, John Joseph Lane, or JoJo, as everyone called him.

My dad died in a car accident when I was nine. I then developed a burning curiosity to find out everything about his life and his family. My mother had packed away most of my father's things. I looked through them and found them lacking in giving me any clue about who he really was. So, when I spent time with my grandma, I looked to her for information.

I rummaged through my father's old room and that was where I first found pictures of my dad's father, JoJo.

Grandma always spoke highly of JoJo. He was a good father, a good husband. They were in love and happy. My dad, as a boy, had adored JoJo.

"What happened to him?" I remembered asking grandma. "Did he die?"

She was in her seventies then but had the face of a younger woman. Her smile faded away and her eyes became serious. "He left one day," she said.

"But where did he go?" I pressed on. At the age of nine, I didn't understand the concept of separation, abandonment, or heartbreak.

"I don't know, honey. You see, he had lost his job and we were struggling," she explained. "Sometimes, I think he just, you know, maybe went off somewhere and decided to disappear."

I remember being shocked and horrified at the prospect. As a child I didn't know that people could just vanish. Except for kids who were stolen. But adults? They were never supposed to disappear.

After that, I never asked any more pointed questions about JoJo, but sometimes grandma would make a remark that would give me a snippet of information. His favorite meal was meatloaf with mashed potatoes, peas, and yeast rolls. He was a good dancer. When my grandma was pregnant, JoJo knew it was going to be a boy. He was so excited to have a son.

Then he left when my dad was eight years old. It made no sense. I asked my mom about the whole situation later. She just shrugged. According to my dad, he fell asleep one night and the next morning JoJo was gone.

I think of this as I rake the leaves into piles. I start at the perimeter of the yard, and I am working my way to the center. I am out of shape and am starting to sweat despite the cool temperature.

One last drags of the rake across the ground and I am going to go in and rest. I cannot believe my 97-year-old grandmother raked these leaves. My thoughts are interrupted when I realize that the rake is stuck on something.

I can't seem to pull it toward me, so I lift it up and that is when I see that the rake is tangled with a leather strap.

Bending down, pushing the leaves and grass away, I realize that the strap is connected to something that is buried. I pull harder on the strap, and I feel something give way, but it is deep. Retrieving a small garden trowel from the shed, I dig until I can make out the top of a leather bag.

After a few minutes of pulling and digging, I got the item out. It is an old leather purse, stiff, scratched and caked with mud.

The clasp on top is an old clasp. The kind with two metal pieces that wrap around each other and make a snap sound when they are forced closed. It is rusty but after some effort, I managed to pry the purse open.

Looking down into the black plastic lining, I see that the purse is empty except for a bundle wrapped in wax paper. The paper is brittle when I unfold it. Inside I found a large brown stained envelope, and within it another smaller envelope. I open it to find even more wax paper and finally a thick bundle of folded notebook paper tied with string. I untie the string and open the paper.

It seems to be a letter of some kind. The first page has only one sentence: "Dear JoJo I am so sorry" is written in my grandma's precise cursive script.

At that moment, I heard a car pull into the driveway in front of the house. The hospice aide is here. I feel panicked. I go into the house, stopping in the kitchen.

For some reason, I feel as if no one should see me with these papers. I tuck everything underneath the kitchen sink before I open the front door to greet the hospice aide.

Grandma wakes up when we enter her bedroom. She is confused when she sees the aide put the blood pressure cuff around her upper arm.

"What are you doing!?" she snaps at the aide.

The aide's name tag says LeVonna. She smiles at my grandma. "I'm just checking on you Miss Lane, just kicking the tires and looking under the hood." My grandma laughs. "I think my transmission is going," she says.

We all laugh. "Maybe so, but your motor is still running, grandma," I tell her.

After LeVonna left, I put on the kettle and take some warm chamomile tea up to the bedroom, but grandma has already gone back to sleep. It won't be long now, I think.

I pull the papers out from under the sink. I look at that first page again, "Dear JoJo I am so sorry". I flip to the next page to read on. My grandmother's handwriting was unmistakable.

'Date: Monday, November 25, 1963

JoJo, you are gone. I know where you are, and I cannot tell anyone, and I cannot keep it in. So, I will tell you the pages. Only the pages will know. I will write this. I will bury it deeply. Deep in the ground, deep in me.

JoJo lost his job three months ago. He was working for Wilhelm's furniture. He had been there for years, but then the owner died, and the place shut down, laid everyone off.

At first, we weren't worried, but then when JoJo started trying to find work, he couldn't. No one was hiring, not the factories, not the stores. Then we got behind on rent.

The landlord said he would work with us, but then the gas bill went unpaid and got turned off. It was getting colder. I dressed in layers; I dressed our boy in layers. I scraped together meals of salt and pepper and butter and rice.

Finally, we got into a fight. I told JoJo, he was no kind of man, no kind of father, that couldn't even feed his child, couldn't even keep him warm.

JoJo, I will never forget your face when you left that night.'

I looked up for a moment. So, there had been an argument, but that hardly explained the fact that JoJo was never seen or heard from again.

I flipped to the third page, hoping to find answers. Grandma had written this page later.

'Date: Wednesday, November 26, 1963

JoJo, you came back. You left but you came back, and you had money. A big pile of cash. It looked funny. It was smeared with something and then I realized that it was blood. You were bleeding, from your side but you said it was nothing.

You told me to hide the money. Use a bit of it to buy food and pay the gas bill and rent but hide the rest.

Then you said you had to leave. JoJo, you said you were going to go to our cave, the one we used to go to when we were courting. You will be back in a few days. If anyone asked, I was to say that you were out of town, looking for work. That you would be back. But You Never Came Back.'

Within the handwritten pages was a newspaper clipping. It was about a robbery of a tavern two counties away.

I read the clipping carefully, suspecting what it had to do with JoJo.

The headline was big and bold in all capital letters:

'ROBBERY GONE WRONG, ONE DEAD, MONEY MISSING'

'Officials are still trying to piece together what happened at Big Al's Tavern on the night of November 23, 1963. The tavern was reportedly not very busy and the last customer who left at midnight reported seeing the owner, Al Harvey cleaning the counter as he usually did at closing time.

The next morning, Big Al would be dead on the floor of the tavern and a trail of blood led out the door. Unfortunately, it was impossible to track further because of heavy rain during the night and early morning hours. Eyewitness accounts state that a man in a red-checked shirt was seen running into the woods behind the tavern.'

So, JoJo, desperate to provide for his family, had committed a robbery. It was almost heroic, but I couldn't push away the grim thought that he had somehow killed a man in the process.

Looking down into the bundle of paper, I see another newspaper clipping.

'BIG AL PUT UP A FIGHT'

'Sherriff Earnest Glenn stated in an interview that officers have been able to figure out what probably happened during the robbery at Big Al's Tavern on the fateful night of November 23, just one day after the assassination of our president.

While the nation was in mourning, someone entered Big Al's just after closing to rob the tavern. Big Al was no pushover, however, and had other plans for the perpetrator. From the amount of blood spilled it looked as if the unknown assailant was stabbed deeply at least once.

Unfortunately, Big Al was injured during the struggle and died of a head injury sustained when fell and hit the wooden bar top on the way down. Sherriff Glen made this statement: 'Wherever the assailant is, he will be looking for a hospital, he is going to have to get patched up somewhere.

We will find him. It doesn't matter if Al died from the fall, we will be looking at murder charges.'

The next page was dated Friday, December 6, 1963. It was written in grandma's handwriting:

'Dear JoJo, I went to the cave. I know you told me to wait but I went to the cave where we used to go, where we spent so many hours talking with each other, loving each other.

I found you there my darling. At first, I was relieved to see you sitting against the wall. Then I saw the blood that had poured out of you, your eyes unseeing, your skin marble cold. And there you were in front of me and gone at the same time. I will tell no one. I love you and I will tell no one what you did or where you are. Good-bye my love.'

After that she had written one more thing: $5576.00.

I guessed that must have been how much JoJo had gotten from the robbery.

I was stunned. It was all here, the solution to our family mystery. JoJo had committed a robbery to keep his family fed and warm. A fight between him and the owner of the business followed. JoJo was seriously injured; the other man was killed in the struggle. JoJo managed to make it home, give grandma the money and take refuge in a cave, where he died of his injuries.

Upstairs, I hear my grandma stirring. I hid the papers underneath the couch cushion and run upstairs. She is out of bed and so confused.

"I need to get to work." She tells me.

"Where?" I ask.

She is annoyed with me. "The drugstore, silly! Who ARE you anyway?"

"I'm your granddaughter, Maddie." I answer.

She laughs. "I don't have a granddaughter, I'm only eighteen!"

I realize that her mind is somewhere back in time before the tragedy of JoJo.

"Do you have a boyfriend?" I ask slyly.

Grandma smiles again. "His name is JoJo; he is so handsome! He takes me courting in the cave behind the old Myers farm sometimes, we can be alone there."

Then the smile fades. "Where am I?" she asks.

I tell her she is home and I help her back to bed.

That is the last time she spoke. Grandma died the following night.

I hid the letters at my apartment and never told anyone about them.

It took me a few days looking through old property records to figure out where the old Myers farm had been. A mall sits there now, but it is long since closed and abandoned.

The woods behind it are still intact. I waited for the weather to warm up and decided to hike out there.

I found the cave. There was graffiti and a bit of trash near the entrance. Inside, it was dark and cool. It went deep into the side of the mountain.

I had brought a long spool of fishing line, attached it to a tree outside and unwound it as I walked deeper into the dark abyss. I didn't know how big it was and I didn't want to lose my way. I moved my flashlight through the dark and when I saw nothing, I kept walking.

Then I noticed a shaft of sunlight coming through a crack in the rocks. I walked toward this light and found myself in a separate chamber.

At first, I thought it was empty too. Then I spotted the still human figure sitting propped against a large boulder. The bones of JoJo Lane still sit. He still wears the black cowboy boots, the blue jeans and red-checked button-up shirt he put on one morning in November of 1963.

The skull grins and a skeletal hand is reaching out toward me. I kneel and look at the empty eye sockets. 'Found you,' I say. JoJo doesn't reply. I sat with my grandfather for a while. The cave is still, the sunlight begins to fade.

I reach over to hold the skeletal hand. I think long and hard what to do. Should I alert the police? Should I make an anonymous report? Should I tell my sister and my mom?

Then I realized, I don't have to decide today. He has been here for decades. A few more years won't hurt. I will leave him alone for now. As I rise from the floor of the cave, I can almost feel him looking at me. I turn around, half expecting him to animate, to tell me not to go yet.

The skeleton still sits. Expecting nothing. Asking nothing.

I tell JoJo goodbye and turn to follow my fishing line through the dark cave and back into the present, leaving JoJo to sit where the past had left him.

Chapter 12

Partners in Crime

My typing was annoyingly loud. I remember as a child I used to wake up at the brink of dawn and log into my computer to use this online typing test that I was obsessed.

The typing test showed how fast you could type with WPM. The only problem is that now my typing speed has increased but I can't seem to type quieter.

My siblings used to hate this, so they threw pillows at me until I was banished to the living room.

The little runts. Even if we didn't get along much as kids, I still really miss them. My older sister is in Australia right now, living the free healthcare life!

My younger sister is out and about in Montana doing who knows what. I guess that's one of the depressing parts of adulthood no one tells you about; living away from the people that make home.

"No!" I shouted. I have just lost this ridiculously obsessive snake game on my laptop. I cautiously checked to see if anyone was watching me from my cubicle. I was supposed to be working on finances for the company. If you saw the excel sheet I was working on, you'd have the same reaction!

"Ada, may I speak to you for a moment, please?" I switched tabs as quickly as I could and calmly turned around. Growing up in a strict household really teaches you how to lie and normally act no matter the circumstances.

I smiled. "Of course." She led me down the prison-like hall and took a right. We stood in front of her office. Her office was exactly like the rest of the building; dull and boring.

She carefully took out keys from her skirt pocket, I needed a skirt pocket desperately, and fumbled around with the lock. Ever since the break-in three months ago, she's put a lock on her door to make sure it never happens again. Talking about being ready.

The robber broke into her office, there was no lock, so the robber technically didn't break-in, and stole her MacBook, two dress suits from her closet, her pure diamond engagement ring, and her pair of raycon wireless earbuds.

It was a catastrophe. Some of the evidence suggested that it was an employee. I have some suspects in mind, but the last time I tried bringing it up, my boss just shooed the idea off and insisted that she trusts her workers.

After fumbling with the doorknob for a solid thirty seconds, she opened the door to her office. No employee has been in here since the break-in, so I looked around, trying to get used to her office again. It was still as bland as ever.

"Take a seat, Ada," the boss said. I cautiously sat in the white leather rolling chair that sat across from her. She placed her hands onto the desk. "As you know, we have a holiday party on the 20th every year." Oh no. "I know you don't celebrate Christmas or any winter holidays, but I would love for you to come.

You've just worked so hard these past few months and I want you to relax, sit back, and enjoy for once." I wanted to tell her that my idea of relaxation is sitting in my one-room apartment living room, cuddled onto the couch with my cat Gasper with no human interaction and a cup of hot chocolate.

"I would love to!" I said instead.

She smiled. "We're doing a potluck this year, so if you can, could you bring your mother's samosas? If not, it is totally fine." I would love to bring my mom's samosas; however, my mom and I aren't exactly in contact anymore. She lives extremely close to my apartment so it's a miracle that we haven't bumped into each other.

Every time I see her face I'm reminded of my terrible teenage years. She used to yell at me no matter what I did. I was working a part-time job, had an IB diploma, president of SGA and other clubs, kept up with my social life, and managed to join two sports teams at my school.

Despite all of that, she still didn't have the slightest grace on my mental deprivation. I was yelled at every morning the second I woke up for my grades. You want to know what my grades were? I had an A+ in five of my classes, an A- in one, and a C in one class. Those are actually pretty good grades considering everything else in my life.

I now understand that my mom just wanted the best, but those few years of my life were absolute hell.

Instead, I smiled. "I'll try my best to bring those samosas, but I'm not completely sure because I've been very busy lately." That was a lie.

"Great!"

Sigh. I was cuddled onto my cream-colored couch with my cat Gasper and was having an amazing time until I remembered my mom's samosas. The holiday party was a day away and I hadn't even called my mom. Ok. I can do this. My heart was beating rapidly,

I grabbed my purse from the doorknob in my room and put my mom's phone number on the dial. Bzz-bzz. That ringing sound my phone makes didn't help calm my nerves at all.

Someone picked up the phone.

"Hello?" my mom said. I haven't heard her voice in ages. Nightmares of my teenage years began flooding back. I've already come this far; I can't back down now.

I gulped. "H-hi mama, it's me, Ada." I heard a gasp on the other side of the phone.

"Ada, honey," mom squeaked. "Why haven't you called me? I've tried calling you all these years and you haven't answered or picked up. What's going on?"

Oh no. I could feel tears burning at the back of my eyes. "Why are you acting like you don't remember?" I snapped. There is no way I'm letting her forget.

"Honey, I'm sorry. I regret it. I do. I just really need to see my daughter again."

It was silent for a few seconds before I spoke. "I'm coming over."

After talking to my mom for God knows how long, we went shopping for the ingredients you need in samosas. I'll admit, I was a little tense at first. I thought she'd be madder or start yelling again, but instead I felt peaceful. I haven't spent time with people in a while and it felt nice to know I had someone who cared.

After frying the samosas and putting them into a woven basket, I headed back home with my Honda CRV.

Once I got home, I hastily put the samosas into the warmer so that they wouldn't turn stale the next day. I checked my pink watch from Five-below, I know, cheap! 10:00pm?? I thought. I really need to get to sleep.

I changed into my pajamas, closed the light in the living room before running back to my bedroom so that the dark demons wouldn't catch me. As I closed my eyes and fell into a deep sleep, I dreamt of scenarios where the party would turn out to be as horrible as I expected it to be.

I woke up to blurry vision and eye crust. Rubbing my eyes, I checked my clock. 9:30am. Oh no. The party was at 11:00am. Shoot.

I quickly hurled myself out of bed. No time to fold. I brushed my teeth, did my morning prayers, and ran to the closet in less than 10 minutes.

Hmm. What should I wear? I thought. Not like there's many options. I grabbed a simple dress. It went up to my ankles and was sage green with puffy sleeves at the sides. I threw on a cream-colored hijab and ran out the door with my keys in hand. I started up the engine then realized I forgot something. Oh no. The samosas.

I ran as fast as the laws of physics could take me without locking my car. Who cares, anyways? It's not like a thief would want to steal my three-year old starburst I had kept in my car.

As I made it into my house, I opened the warmer, grabbed the samosas, and headed out into my car. Not caring what the police thought, I accelerated at 40 miles per hour and finally arrived at the party.

As I walked in, I almost didn't recognize the prison-like workplace. Holiday decorations filled up the room and made it look almost magical. Oh no. Everyone here was wearing red, green, or white.

Great, now I'm sticking out like a sore thumb. Thankfully, most people were already here so the attention wasn't turned to me. If I creeped around everyone, maybe I could get away without talking to anyone-

"Oh my gosh? Ada?!" Mary shouted. Oh no.

I plastered on my lovely fake smile. "Hey!"

"I'm so happy you finally made it to a holiday party! How's it been going?" Mary said, smiling. She was a co-worker of mine that I hated for no reason. Okay, maybe there was a reason. I was jealous. She always has the perfect outfits, a perfect smile, perfect skin, perfect hair, perfect body, perfect personality. Everything about her was better.

"I'm doing great! How about you?"

Mary frowned. "I broke up with my boyfriend, but you know it's all good. I guess he wasn't meant for me." She shrugged.

"I'm sorry that happened," I said, standardly. As Mary and I chatted it up, some of my other co-workers began to join the conversation and before I knew it, I was overcoming one of my greatest fears, social interaction. It was…. surprisingly great.

Mary was wearing a red dress suit with a black stain on the breast pocket. Hm. That's weird. The boss had a dress suit exactly like that with a black stain at the breast pocket. Weird. As if my mind had somehow been read, the boss came up to the two of us. Mary tensed up a little.

"Hellooo ladies!" she said, holding a red cup of booze. Oh god, she is drunk. "I adore that suit you're wearing, Mary. It looks so familiar!"

Mary awkwardly smiled. "Y-yeah! I got this at Macy's!" I guess Mary had been the one I've been suspecting the whole time. I knew something was up with her. She was the culprit of the office robbery.

Slowly, I tapped Mary on the shoulder and led her into the hallway. Thankfully, the boss was too drunk to notice.

"What is it?" Mary said, confused.

I gaped at her like it was obvious. "You're wearing the stolen dress suit." That was a little too blunt.

"I don't know what you're talking about," she lied. "I bought this by myself at Macy's."

Rolling my eyes, I said, "The receipt?"

"I don't carry it wherever I go, silly," Mary said. "And besides, I saw you stealing all those donuts she used to buy. If you keep my secret, I'll keep yours."

Oh shoot. She's good. "Deal." We shook hands firmly.

"I guess you could literally call us partners in crime," she winked. We both cracked up even if that was one of the cheesiest things a person could say.

I smiled. "Partners in crime."

Both girls returned to the party and told tales about the dish the brought to the party....

Ada got very popular talk about her samosa....

She explains were it originated which is as follows:

It is not clear where samosas originate, many dishes of Indian origin were named foreign names after the conquest of the Muslims.

Samosas which are deep fried and triangular may have origins in the Indian subcontinent.

Samsa of central Asia were essentially pies, i-e baked in oven and not deep fried, in central Asia, samosas are never deep fried, whereas in India they are always deep fried.

The pastry folio of Indians involves a different method of preparation compared to the pastry folio in the middle east, which is still practiced today.

Chapter 13

The Crocodile

The Crocodile was becoming a legend very fast. A regionally popular band was making the charts with a driving narcocorrido about "Los Dientes Del Cocodrilo," and his bloody exploits on behalf of the Cartel in Colombia.

The rising star of Colombia's Golden Triangle thus had bristled about meeting in this filthy side-street marisqueria in the tiny backwater of San Felipe. He preferred the gran entrada, the splashy entrance, the spotlight, the erotic perfume of mingled adoration and terror. No audience this afternoon.

With El Chapo Mejias out of circulation, El Cocodrilo had dispatched his gente nueva to noisily dispose of random local cops and wannabe gangsters who claimed cartel juice.

He clogged major boulevards and plazas with carjacked vehicles to impede military or police invasion and divert attention away from the actual stash houses and tiendita, a grocery store, where food was sold.

With the help of his cyber-savvy nephew Tio, The Crocodile had embraced social networking and channeled the power of the flash mob to confound the federales and keep la familia's brand on the public radar.

Tio had discouraged his uncle from launching an online shop for Hecho En Cocodrilo gear, but across Colombia, the appearance of the family's signature croc-skinned boots and Lacoste polos elicited terror, reverence, and bottomless peyote.

The young narcos had given Luis Rodriguez and friends immeasurable street credibility, and the folk clucked in glory disdain while savoring the company's most promising opening had added their reptilian logo to his stage swagger.

El Cocodrilo wished that someday to the glory that came with being de jefe. As he had pointed out in a PowerPoint, Tio's prepared for the Colombians, the cartels had transformed the Colombia economy, pumped new blood into a sagging sector, ignited new pride in a population embarrassingly dependent on the norteamericano tourist dollar.

If a little blood must be shed, it was for the greater good. The Crocodile hand-delivered PCs and cartel-logoed sports gear to rural schools, provided even minor foot soldiers with lavish weddings, quinceanera, and, when necessary, funerals. Giving back, El Cocodrilo stressed, was the cornerstone of corporate responsibility.

He greeted his child server with a dazzling display of indeed very reptilian dental work. The boy attempted to return the gesture as he juggled carnitas and camerones, as if the obese crocodile in the porkpie hat might snap up the shrimp and a few of his digits with one bipolar flourish.

"Como te llama?" El Cocodrilo inquired soothingly. The boy, whose face echoed his grandfather's strong Yaqui bloodline, averted his eyes from the grim men about the table. The Crocodile assumed the muchacho de servicio was dumbstruck by the unexpected humility of such a great man. What had Whitney Houston once said?

"Adrian," the boy managed as he uncomfortably adjusted the platters. Carlos Ramirez had very reluctantly but prudently dispatched the 9-year-old, packing Adrian's beguiling 15-year-old sister Luz off to the market in the city. Carlos knew from tragic experience that The Crocodile and his merry band preferred red meat and tender female flesh.

"An industrious young man," El Cocodrilo proclaimed. The smile faded a notch. "Come on; we're starving."

Adrian hastily distributed the platters, bowed, and crossed calmly to the kitchen to collapse into the wooden chair beside his grandfather's flattop. The Crocodile tucked into his shrimp, looking up irritably as Tio ignored his own steaming plate of pork.

"Que hay?" he rumbled with an agitated swig of the city.

The handsome young techno whiz shrugged. "I got a server address for our blogger, and from there, I can get a name and address. But, with respect, I must ask again if this is really a good idea. To take the war, this war, to the States?"

The Crocodile's sister Lucy occupied a hallowed niche alongside Santa Marta, but her son relied too heavily on his blood ties and cyberskills, and Tio's mouth someday would write a check his uncle was unwilling to cover.

Maybe it was the shrimp, The Crocodile merely shrugged. "Bloggers and Tweeters and hackers have no respect for our economic freedom, for progress. They sow chaos, stand in the way of the national welfare. We let this continue, we will lose the respect of the people."

The Crocodile paused, awaiting his nephew's inevitable plea for "reason." But Tio stared into his uncle's bloodshot eyes with an unnerving intensity. "You got something to say, college boy?" the drug lord demanded, his color rising.

Tio's shining black eyes burned as his lips slackened into a mocking grin, and El Crocodile's overburdened chair shrieked on the tiles. Then the narcotrafficker saw it -- Tio's pupils now consumed the espresso irises that had hypnotized many a club girl into surrendering her dubious virtue.

"Boy, you are fucking crazy?" The Crocodile wheezed. "I told you, no using on the job!"

Tio's lips parted, and a bubbly foam trickled down his squared jaw. His uncle's wrath dissolved into concern. He turned to Heriberto, an astonishingly stupid but indestructible third cousin-cum-enforcer who'd been shoveling stuff during the mounting familial conflict.

"There's a doctor we use, Morales, a few doors away I think," The Crocodile growled. "Get him here, now. Vamanos!"

Roberto nodded and fell face-first into his fried pork. The lieutenant to his right swiveled slightly, and his tartar-coated tongue emerged to absently lick chile sauce from his mustache as The Crocodile's muscle began to drown noisily.

The fifth diner, a hitman skilled in managing Internet snitches, hummed Daniel Rivera's playful theme to The Simpsons as his now-autonomous digits thumped non-existent keys on the sauce-spattered tabletop.

El Cocodrilo felt an icy jab of revelation. Old Oscar had poisoned their food on behalf of one of the rivals familia. His tingling fingers fumbled his Herstal five-seven free of his jacket holster. He turns over his chair, and his legs buckled beneath him. Santos would-be jefe landed on his ass, and he screamed in impotent rage.

"Zapato" The Crocodile bellowed at the elderly assassin in the kitchen. "Zapatos!!"

Slicing onions for the evening crowd, Carlos Ramirez though about why El Cocodrilo might be demanding shoes and how he might meet such a demand.

Minutes later, as the restaurant was flooded with heavily armed federales and norteamericanos, Carlos's problems were both resolved and multiplied.

She rose, grunting slightly. Strenuous, repetitive labor and an affection for chocolate and Mr. Cruz had strained the cartilage in her knees and honed the plantar fasciitis in her arches. She was 24, felt twice that. But now, joyful warmth spread through her overworked limbs.

The windowless chamber was illuminated by a hundred teardrop flames. Dead eyes stared at the mutely joyful young woman. A doorbell began to sound in rhythmic cycles, and she sought the other source of illumination, the screen of a Samsung Galaxy hours out of the box.

As instructed, she ended the incoming call with the trembling punch of a rough index finger. She began respectfully to extinguish the flames, murmuring a benediction and a prayer of contrition.

She'd learned the rough way that pride not only was a cardinal sin but also a potentially fatal failing. Even as she snuffed the last of the dollar store votives, she savored the company of saints and monsters.

The Mauve Shirts tensed slightly as the young man went about restocking Aquafina and Diet Coke and unwrapping a huge platter of chocolate chip cookies provided by grateful Best Western management.

Normally, in any room in Fountain Hills, Dontae was the invisible man, Ellison's, not Wells', and the attention now was frightening. Up on the screen was the image of a huge, wrinkled hog, surrounded by Chinese guys taking notes.

I didn't want to know how THAT fit into this scenario, or for that matter the slender sister at the end of the table, who accepted Dontae's fraternal nod with a frosty smile. Dontae's deductive instinct ebbed, and he rattled out with a tub of melted ice.

"So," Danzer continued as the assembled "commodity analysts" attacked the cookies. "We've been accumulating on-the-ground data on a potentially tremendous untapped energy source. Well, untapped until recently. That's why I invited our friend from the DOJ to join us today.

Deputy Administrator Michael Ramos, as many of you know, oversees the DEA. If you've read the papers or watched CNN over the last several days, you may be aware that the DEA has scored a major victory in the war on the cartels."

Ramos looked uncertainly to Danzer, who smiled encouragement. "Not that I'm underplaying the significant blow dealt the Colombia Cartel with the apprehension of Manuel 'El Cocodrilo' Amandares and several of his key lieutenants. The…unusual…nature of our offensive against Amandares could mark a monumental turning point in the war against narcotrafficking."

"Unusual?" the deputy CIA director murmured with the same hypothermic smile she'd granted the hotel busboy. "I'd understood DEA and the Federales caught The Crocodile and his friends with their pants down in some small-town dump."

Ramos nodded. "This raid had been in the works for a week, after our inside man found out Almandares and his top guys were holding a clandestine meeting to deal with cybervigilantes. This presented a prime opportunity to strike at the executive heart of the organization. As it turned out, force proved unnecessary."

"Charlie, if I may," Danzer suggested. "By the time DEA entered the scene, El Crocodrilo and his friends were dead or nearly so from severe cerebrovascular insult. The Crocodile is in a vegetative state under federal custody. His nephew Tio somehow forgot the complex process of breathing."

"Please tell me the DEA didn't deploy biological agents against foreign nationals," the CDC rep drawled.

"Absolutely not," Ramos stammered.

"Well," Danzer shrugged. "He is technically correct. And while Alovar was innocent of any complicity in these men's deaths, his family's fortunes and The Crocodile's fate were inextricably intertwined."

Ramos took up the lagging narrative. "Almendras' nephew wasn't above using his family's rep or drugs to take what he wanted. Carlos had a niece, 14 at the time, who accompanied a cousin to a street festival in Medellin.

She disappeared, and the cousin had the local cops searching everywhere for her. They found the girl a few hours later in a hotel the Cartel frequently used. She'd been sexually assaulted and couldn't remember anything except a conversation with a young guy who'd considerately bought her a soda."

"Roofied," the CIA deputy stated grimly.

"They take the girl, we'll call her Jenny, to the hospital, do a kit, and get a description down to the assailant's crocodile boots. Then the rape kit vanishes, hotel clerk can't remember his own shoe size, and the cousin, who's been screaming for justice, is found up in the hills, tongue cut out and shoved"

"All right," DOD rasped. "Where are we going with this?"

"The Ramirez pack Jenny off to some relatives here in the California metro area. Got her a job at a packing plant in San Diego, but ICE rounded her up with a dozen other undocumented.

Just before her removal proceedings, Dr. Diaz and the San Diego archdiocese intervened on the girl's behalf."

Diaz waved Ramos down. "The family noted the potential threat to the poor girl where she returned to San Rosario, or her current location disclosed.

Fortunately, Operation Streamline's deportation show trials in California were beginning to generate considerable negative press."

"And just how did this unfortunate child come to your attention?" the CIA deputy murmured.

"One of my project associates had become aware of the young girl's dilemma, as well as her very unusual history. A relative related an interesting anecdote of their shared childhood in San Rosario, an anecdote that incidentally turns up in various forms on several websites.

"The incident occurred when they were roughly six or seven years of age, following the death of a much-beloved great-uncle during an confrontation at the local cantina. The extended family gathered at Carlos Ramirez's café for the wake, coffin on a table surrounded by candles and herbs and a massive spread.

"As Ramirez offers a toast to the decedent, the coffin begins first to sway, then to rock. Candles flicker out randomly. Bottles fly from the shelves behind Carlos's bar.

Music explodes from Carlos's kitchen radio, and a family member finds every shelf in the pantry vibrating. Then, as suddenly as the melee began, it ends, leaving a child's voice reciting what sounded like the close of a prayer. As 'Juanita' concludes, she looks up, smiles, and apologizes for 'the trouble.'"

"At about the same time, Raul, and Mauricio Vasquez, who had been charged in the beating death of Great-Uncle Hervey, were found in their cell, throats torn out.

It was determined they had eviscerated themselves. Their irrational actions were consistent with cerebrovascular disruption like that suffered by Almendras and his, er, employees.

Fortunately, we have family video of the occurrence at Ramirez's café. If you all could pull up the file, you were emailed this morning?"

"Holy shit," NSA muttered aptly, 10 minutes later.

Diaz nodded. "We were able to decipher young Jenny's recitation. Psalm 137."

The deputy director smiled mirthlessly. "'Our Lord, punish the Edomites. Because the day Jerusalem fell, they shouted, 'Completely destroy the city! Tear down every building!' You're seriously suggesting this child brought the wrath of God down on her great-uncle's killers?"

"I would suggest that what you've witnessed is the release of a massive level of high-frequency potential energy," Diaz replied coolly. "The 'poltergeist' event at the café was merely the byproduct. Like a laser with defective optics."

"Or a school science project that winds up vaporizing the gym," the spy chief smiled.

Diaz matched her predatory smirk. "One that's since been replicated with far greater precision. I just shipped you all another e-mail, with a second video file."

This one was a split screen. Carlos's café was empty save a circle of clumsily dressed men at the largest table beyond the bar. The right screen was darker, grainier.

Hundreds of light points wavered in what looked to be little more than a maintenance closet lined with metal racks. What the shelves held was the most compelling feature of this Blair Witch footage.

Sharp beaks, claws, wings, teeth. Goggling toadlike orbs, black alien slits, feline and lupine pupils, eyed stalks. Dragons and golem and katsina and bulbously erotic Paleolithic "Venus figures," a familiar figure on a cross.

"It helps our girl achieve the desired mental state," Diaz lied....

A door on the single bare wall swung open and a blocky female entered. She took a stool as the light balance corrected, her back to the camera. Her head dipped, and a young monotone voice began to chant in Spanish as, on the other screen, a young boy warily bore a mammoth tray toward the party.

Digital time stamps on both screens were synched to the second. As the split screen froze on armed men swarming the cafe, the deputy director wheeled. "If this is to be believed, you're admitting to federally sanctioned execution. Diaz, you've made all of us accessories."

Diaz smiled. "To the telekinetic removal of a major narcoterrorism? No, I simply invited you here today to reveal the long-missing link between physics and genetics, the quantum energy of the human consciousness, a crucial validation of Einstein and Schrodinger's unified theories."

"All to whack a drug lord," NSA muttered....

"Imagine conducting a surgical strike against a terrorist target without drone miscalculations or surplus human collateral." Diaz said. He slipped his slim laptop deftly into its RFID-impervious case. "You have much to process at this point, and I will look forward to your response."

Grinning, Diaz found the boys room, then continued down a side hallway and out into the mellowing late afternoon sun. A female figure was silhouetted beside his low-slung vintage Mercedes convertible.

"Well, Janet," he sang. "I thought the group had reconvened."

Deputy CIA Director Janet Martinez shook her head indulgently. "I feel like a mojito."

Without a word, she retrieved a roll of towels and a spray bottle from underneath the Fast Fill's scarred counter and moved to the front of the register.

Luckily, the Plexiglas sheeting the manager had installed for placebo security had largely shielded her from the splatter of hot toffee macchiato.

She would have to launder her royal Blue FF Express apron that night for tomorrow's shift, but the plastic had taken the impact.

He hadn't looked the type, spotless black Lexus in the slot nearest the door, salt-and-pepper snowbird golfer in a teal Lacoste polo and creamily draped slacks bisecting his paunch. Of course, there wasn't really a type these days.

The snowbird's face clouded, and his fist tightened around his receipt as Luis, the Pepsi vendor, gave her a hearty shout-out as he wheeled his dolly back into the sun.

A California Power worker in for his daily Dew and dog tried to intervene, first in his customer service tone, and then angrily as the man began showering the small, blocky clerk with racial epithets, f-bombs, and a general screed on the declining state of White America.

The snowbird concluded by whipping his beverage at the clerk, hurling a different charming epithet at the worker, and storming out.

"I got the motherfucker's plate," the worker growled. "Man, sorry," he hastily apologized, registering the first shock the woman had expressed and gently wresting the roll and bottle from her.

"I can reach better let me get it. You just call the cops. Asshole, man could that seriously burnt you."

The clerk shook her head with a smile. "No es necesario. Gracias."

"But" the lanky lineman objected.

"Rezaré por él." She pressed her palms together and closed her eyes.

Comprehending, the worker grinned. "Well, all I got to say, Jenny, is you're a lot nicer than I'd be."

Chapter 14

Police Stories

Let's talk about the training police officer get. I would like to, at this time, talk about the Police Academy.

In the states and Puerto Rico, the Police Academy trains their young cops basically the same. The training is awesome....

The Academy is somewhat a game. The new recruits learn a lot with the many Police Stories. Some are new and others are old stories.

There are always missions, and new locations to investigate. It is interesting because young officers will get the whole picture from senior police officers as well as young ones. Still, the inexperienced trainees will get plenty information. Remember that they are just learning to be cops.

Let's look at this scenario:

Another day at the police academy goes wrong when unrest breaks out in the city. To make matters worse, a "rat" who works with the local mafia has turned up at the police station. Of course, only two student cops can defy all the trouble!

The police academy will inspire future SWAT teams...

A fresh take on top-down shooters with an emphasis on tactics where decisions must be made in a split second. Rescue hostages, neutralize criminals and defuse bombs in single-player or co-op mode. The recruits at this point will learn that shooting first is not the best decision!

New missions and locations, plus the police academy training ground. Help young Rick and John become brutal cops!

The Surrender System allows you to apprehend the suspects without resorting to violence. Fire a warning shot near them or engage them in melee combat - those are just some of the ways you can make them submit.

Issue commands to your fellow cop Rick Jones. Make sure to use him wisely - and who knows, he might save your life in return.

Randomly placed criminals, hostages and evidence make every level run unique. The placement changes every time you restart, leading to interesting new situations and opportunities.

As a law enforcement officer, you will have access to end-of-the-line police equipment, such as under-the-door cameras, door blast charges and many others.

Various types of lawbreakers, from small petty criminals to well organized gangs and terrorists. Each type has not only unique weapons, but different behavior and shooting skill.

Complex Tactical Gameplay: Try not to get spotted, don't waste bullets, regularly check your surroundings, and make sure to take criminals down quietly.

All your actions are scored in real time. Playing aggressively won't get you a high enough result to start the next mission - so keep that in mind!

Co-op. Complete mission together for better scores and more fun!

Chapter 15

Crime in Puerto Rico

B efore I write about how horrible crime is in Puerto Rico, I want to tell you about our history. We have come a long way, however, with the return of many Puerto Ricans to the island, they bring with them bad habits...

The Police Department and the Puerto Rico National Guard work together to keep us safe.

Armed forces and Police

Puerto Rico continues to be a strategic site for the U.S. military. For decades the U.S. Navy has occupied a large base at Roosevelt Roads, on the east coast. By 2001 local protests had mounted against the navy's use of a portion of the nearby island of Vieques for its maneuvers, including gunnery and bombing practice, and the federal government, bowing to public pressure, announced plans to halt the bombing.

Drug interdiction in Puerto Rico

Unlike the various municipal, county, and state police forces common in the United States, Puerto Rico has a single, centralized police force, which includes a body of detectives.

Puerto Rico is considered a major transshipment point for illegal drugs from South America to North America, and local and U.S. law enforcement agencies have long been engaged in drug interdiction efforts in the island.

Education

More than nine-tenths of the people are literate. Schooling is compulsory and free for children between the ages of 6 and 16. Although most children complete at least eight years of education, there is a high dropout rate.

About half of Puerto Ricans aged 25 and older are high school graduates, and bachelor's degrees are held by one-seventh of the population. Nearly one-fourth are high school graduates.

Puerto Rico invests heavily in education, nearly one-third of its annual budget notably in vocational and technical programs. The U.S. federal funds also encourage attendance in schools and universities. The main public institution of higher learning is the University of Puerto Rico was founded in 1903, with its main campus at Río Piedras.

Among the several private universities and colleges are the Inter-American University, 1912, which has several campuses, and the Pontifical Catholic University,1948 in Ponce.

Health and welfare

In 1947 the Puerto Rican birth rate was about 43 per 1,000 people, whereas life expectancy at birth was only about 50 years. Health conditions subsequently improved dramatically, approaching the standards of the U.S. states. The life expectancy at birth is now some 79 years for Puerto Rican women and 71 for men.

Major causes of death include heart disease, cancers, diabetes, cerebrovascular diseases, and pneumonia and influenza. Urban clinics and rural health centers provide basic medical care, and the U.S. Medicare and Medicaid programs have contributed to improving health among lower-income residents, as have various other social programs.

In the 1990s the Puerto Rican government initiated financial reforms of the health care system, including privatizing some hospitals and clinics.

The government has long worked to upgrade rural and urban areas with piped water, electricity, and other amenities. It has also improved the housing situation, notably through its Urban Renewal and Housing Corporation, which concentrates on low-income housing projects. A water-treatment system and aqueduct, laid out along the coast from north-central Puerto Rico to San Juan, opened in 2000.

Cultural life

The idealized folk hero of Puerto Rico is the jíbaro, a rustic independent hill-farmer whose status in local song and story is like that of the gaucho of Argentina.

However, modern Puerto Rican cultural life is a blend of North American and Latin, African, and Caribbean forms, as is evident in much of the island's dance, music, art, literature, and sports.

The pre-Columbian Taino culture, which was largely decimated by European colonizers, has had only limited impact on Puerto Rican life and is evident mainly in the use of certain linguistic expressions and words incorporated into the Spanish language, such as hamaca, "hammock", cacique, "chief", and tabaco, "tobacco".

African influences are found in food, music, and art. Music festivals, museums in Ponce and San Juan, and theatrical performances encourage Hispanidad, or Spanish customs. Puerto Ricans have worked to preserve a Latin heritage while welcoming U.S. economic and social novelties, engendering a cultural dilemma that has often catalyzed political debate.

Daily life

Puerto Rican lifestyles have changed rapidly as new technologies, economic opportunities, and patterns of development emerged. The island remains far poorer than the United States, but its growing middle class has adopted living standards that would be familiar to most North Americans.

Some two-thirds of Puerto Rican families own their own homes. Large areas of former farmland have been converted to suburban communities,urbanizations, rural wooden shacks have been replaced by sturdy cement houses equipped with modern appliances.

Cars have increasingly clogged modern highways, particularly during evening rush hours in the San Juan area. A hungry appetite for consumer goods, combined with easy access to credit, prompts shoppers to jam air-conditioned suburban malls that feature U.S. chain stores, fast-food restaurants, and multiplex cinemas.

On most Saturday nights in San Juan, well-dressed young suburbanites crowd the dance floors of nightclubs and hotels. Once the exclusive province of tourists or frequent the bars and cafés of historic Old San Juan.

Puerto Ricans continue to prefer traditional dishes with rice and beans, plantains, and beef, chicken, or pork. However, North American fast-food restaurants that sell hamburgers, pizza, and other fare are growing in popularity, particularly among the young.

Traditional Creole foods include sopa de arroz con pollo, chicken-and-rice soup, sancocho, a beef-and-vegetable stew, tostones, fried plantain slices, flan, and casabe, powdery cakes made from ground cassava, often served with molasses and coconut milk.

Local supermarkets are well stocked with traditional fare as well as frozen and processed foods, which are mainly imported from the United States. Locally produced soft drinks and rums are also popular.

Cultural institutions

Most of Puerto Rico's cultural institutions, including its major universities and libraries, are concentrated in the San Juan area. The Puerto Rican Athenium, Ateneo Puertorriquena; 1876, is a prestigious learned society.

The University of Puerto Rico Library System, 1903, is the island's main library, with more than four million holdings divided among 12 sites. Works by Puerto Rican painters and sculptors are displayed in the Museum of Contemporary Art, 1984, and the Puerto Rican Museum of Art, 2000, which are in San Juan.

Also notable are the Ponce Art Museum, 1959 and the Museum of Religious Art, the latter housed in a 17th-century church in San Germán. The Luis A. Ferré Fine Arts Centre, 1981, in San Juan is the venue for many theatrical and musical events.

Among the island's research centers are the Institute of Puerto Rican Culture, 1955 and the International Institute of Tropical Forestry, 1939. The Arecibo Observatory, 1963–2020, a radio telescope with a 1,000-foot, 305-metre, diameter, was, for most of its life, the largest of its kind in the world. It collapsed in 2020.

Some of the island's earliest inhabitants created polychrome ceramics, amulets, and stone carvings. About 1000 CE the Taino used granite, marble, and other types of stone to carve three-pointed figures with human and animal features; they also produced ceremonial stools, wooden rattles, petroglyphs surrounding their ball courts, and stone-carved ceremonial belts or collars.

During Puerto Rico's colonial period, African slaves formed multicolored coconut-fiber masks for local festivals, a tradition that is still carried on. José de Riverchase y Campeche, 1751–1809, was the island's first major painter.

The most notable 19th-century painters were Ramón Atiles y Pérez and Francisco Oller. More recent artists include Julio Rosado del Valle, Rafael Tufiño, Antonio Martorell, and Augusto Marín.

Literature

Contemporary poets, novelists, short-story writers, and essayists keep alive the traditions of such 19th-century forerunners as novelist Manuel Zeno Gandía, playwright Alejandro Tapia, essayist Eugenio María de Hostos, and poet José Gautier Benítez.

Leading 20th-century and contemporary authors include novelists and short-story writers Abelardo Díaz Alfaro, Enrique Laguerre, Pedro Juan Soto, Emilio Díaz Valcárcel, José Luis González, and Rosario Ferré; poets Julia de Burgos and Luis Palés Matos, whose works reflect Afro-Caribbean influences.

Playwright René Marqués: and poet and playwright Pedro Pietri, who inspired young Puerto Ricans living in New York City, called Nuyoricans, by composing poetry that instilled pride in their culture and heritage.

Performing Arts

Puerto Rican musicians, composers, and actors have made marks far beyond their island's shores, and some have been counted among the world's most famous pop-culture figures.

Notable Puerto Rican stage and screen performers included the Academy Award winners José Ferrer, Rita Moreno, and Benicio Del Toro, as well as Raúl Juliá. Other performers of Puerto Rican descent included Chita Rivera and Jennifer Lopez.

Among 19th-century composers are Manuel Tavárez and Juan Morel Campos, both known for their dance melodies. The popular 20th-century songwriter Rafael Hernández is still revered throughout Latin America.

The Spanish-born cellist Pablo Casals, whose mother was Puerto Rican, moved to the island in 1956 and founded the world-famous classical music festival there that bears his name.

Puerto Rican musicians have included the classical pianist Jesus María Sanromá, opera singers Antonio Paoli and Justino Díaz, and popular musicians Ruth Fernández, Tito Puente, José Feliciano, Cheo Feliciano, Ricky Martin, and Calle 13.

Latin jazz and salsa are enjoyed throughout the island; also popular are merengue, rock, rap, the Afro-Caribbean bomba, and the tambourine-marked plena. Many musical groups preserve jíbaro, folk, music by playing such instruments as the cuatro, a small guitar carved from a single piece of wood, the marímbula, a wooden box on which are mounted tuned metal tongues, the güiro, a percussive gourd that is also a popular decoration, drums, and maracas.

Sports and Recreation

Baseball is Puerto Rico's national sport, and the island has long been a source for U.S. major-league players, including Roberto Clemente, Orlando Cepeda, Juan, "Igor", González, Bernie Williams, Roberto Hernández, Iván Rodríguez, and Leo Gómez. Boxing and basketball are also popular.

Let me also point out that Edwin Rodriguez Morales, was the first Boricua manager in the major league. He is presently the manager of the Leones de Ponce, here in Puerto Rico.

Puerto Rican boxers of note include José Torres, Edwin Rosario, Hector Camacho, and Félix, "Tito", Trinidad.

Cockfighting and Thoroughbred horse racing events, where gambling is permitted, are also well attended. Puerto Rico has competed in the Olympic Games since 1948, and its boxers are frequent contenders for medals.

Puerto Rico observes many of the secular holidays of the United States, and, as elsewhere in Latin America, its municipalities celebrate numerous religious festivals centered on the feast days of patron saints. The Festival of St. John the Baptist, June 24, in San Juan climaxes at midnight when revelers walk backward into the sea, an act said to bring good luck.

Ponce hosts a pre-Lenten Carnival featuring horn-masked celebrants who dance and take part in parades, and the town of Hatillo holds the Carnival-like Festival of the Masks each December 28.

Press and Broadcasting

The commonwealth has a free press, and local and major U.S. newspapers are widely available, as are foreign publications. Puerto Rico has several weekly and daily periodicals, the largest of which are El Nuevo Día, El Vocero de Puerto Rico, and the San Juan Star, which has both English- and Spanish-language editions.

The first radio broadcast in Puerto Rico was made in 1923, and the island now has some 120 AM and FM radio stations, giving it one of the world's highest densities of radio broadcasters. Nearly all broadcasts are in Spanish.

Television was introduced in 1954, and there are now a dozen Spanish-language TV stations, with programming comparable to that shown in the United States.

Puerto Rico also has government radio and television stations, which feature educational and cultural broadcasts. English-language channels and other programming are available via cable television and satellite.

Chapter 16

History of Puerto Rico

The following discussion focuses on Puerto Rican history from the time of European settlement.

The first inhabitants of Puerto Rico were hunter-gatherers who reached the island more than 1,000 years before the arrival of the Spanish. Arawak Indians, who developed the Taino culture, had also settled there by 1000 CE. The clan-based Taino lived in small villages led by a cacique, or chief.

They had a limited knowledge of agriculture but grew such domesticated tropical crops as pineapples, cassava, and sweet potatoes and supplemented their diet with seafood. In the late 15th century 20,000–50,000 Taino lived on Puerto Rico, which they called Borinquen, Borinquén, or Boriken.

The Taino occasionally warded off attacks by their Carib neighbors from islands to the south and east, including the Virgin Islands and Vieques Island.

In 1493 Christopher Columbus left Spain on his second voyage to the Indies with a large expedition of 17 ships and about 1,500 men.

At the island of Guadeloupe, the Spaniards rescued several Taino prisoners whom the Carib had taken from Borinquen, and Columbus agreed to return them to their island. On November 19, 1493, Columbus anchored in a bay on the west coast of Borinquen, which he promptly renamed San Juan Bautista "Saint John the Baptist "and claimed for the Spanish monarchs Ferdinand II and Isabella I.

The expeditionary spent two days on the island before sailing westward to Hispaniola, where they established the first permanent settlement in the New World.

Early settlement

For 15 years San Juan Bautista was neglected except for an occasional visit by a ship putting in for supplies. In 1508 Juan Ponce de León, who had accompanied Columbus and worked to colonize Hispaniola, was granted permission to explore the island.

On the north coast Ponce de León found an exceptionally well-protected bay that could harbor many sailing vessels; on high ground beside the bay, he founded Caparra, the island's first town and the site of its first mining and agricultural operations. By 1521 the town was moved to an islet at the northern end of the harbor and renamed Puerto Rico, "Rich Port".

Through time and common usage, the port became known as San Juan while the name Puerto Rico came to be applied to the whole island.

The Taino soon lost reverence for their Spanish "protectors," who expected the Indians to act as vassals, paying tribute in gold and food as well as accepting instruction in the Christian religion.

Meanwhile, European diseases, to which the Spaniards were largely immune, and maltreatment had begun to devastate the Taino population.

In 1511 the Indians rebelled but had only temporary success against the better-armed Spanish, who again subjugated them. The Spanish subsequently brought Indian slaves from nearby islands and black slaves from Africa to fully staff their placer mines. However, gold production markedly declined after the 1530s, and many of the Europeans migrated elsewhere.

Those who remained set up sugarcane and ginger plantations with their African slaves, but the colony continued to lead a precarious existence. Carib groups from neighboring islands made frequent raids, carrying off food and slaves and destroying property.

Puerto Rico was further ravaged by disease, and it was plundered by French, British, and Dutch pirates. During the mid-16th century French forces repeatedly burned and sacked San Germán, the island's second settlement. Increasing numbers of colonists left the island.

San Cristóbal fortress, San Juan, Puerto Rico

In the second half of the 16th century Spain, recognizing the strategic importance of Puerto Rico, undertook to convert San Juan into a military outpost by using a financial subsidy from the Mexican mines.

Initially they built a fortified palace for the governor called La Fortaleza, "The Fortress", followed by the massive San Felipe del Morro, El Morro castle, which was perfectly located to dominate the narrow entrance to the harbor.

Finally, they added a stronger and larger fortress, San Cristóbal, to the northeast, on the Atlantic side of the city.

In the early 17th century, the city was surrounded by a stone wall 25 feet, 8 meters high and 18 feet, 5 meter regnable.

San Juan: El Morro

In 1595 Sir Francis Drake attacked the city with a sizable fleet but failed to silence its guns. Three years later the British soldier George Clifford, 3rd earl of Cumberland, captured the city but was soon forced to abandon it after his troops fell victim to disease, probably dysentery.

In 1625 the Dutchman Bowdoin Hendrik captured and burned the town but failed to subdue El Morro, where the governor had taken refuge.

San Juan, the most exposed military outpost guarding Spain's New World empire, received political and economic attention from the mother country; however, the island's rural inhabitants, or jíbaros, were typically ignored by Spain and mocked by the residents of San Juan.

The jíbaros thus resisted for themselves and cultivated their own small landholdings. As the French, British, Danish, and Dutch fought over and settled the Lesser Antilles during the 17th and 18th centuries, the colonial authorities of San Juan rarely ventured beyond their walled defenses for fear of buccaneer attacks; however, the jíbaros, ignoring the edicts of Spain, prospered somewhat by trading clandestinely with non-Spanish merchants.

Ginger, hides, sugarcane, tobacco, and cattle from the island were in great demand. The settlers' contact with foreigners did not turn them away from their mother country, as the Spanish crown had feared, instead, they remained loyal and willing to participate in military expeditions.

Liberal Reforms and Regional Turmoil

During the 18th century Spain's Bourbon rulers ordered their colonial representatives to carry out sweeping economic and administrative reforms that promoted trade between Puerto Rico and Spain, stimulated agricultural production, and integrated the island's various military units into a unified command, all to convert Puerto Rico from a financial drain to a major economic asset.

The enlightened despotism of the Spanish Bourbons encouraged Puerto Rico's commercial agriculture. The island's population grew rapidly, from roughly 45,000 in 1765 to more than 103,000 in 1787 and 155,000 in 1800.

By the end of the 18th century there were 34 towns on the island. Among the larger immigrant groups were Canary Islanders, French settlers from Louisiana or Haiti, and Spaniards from Santo Domingo, later the Dominican Republic, which had been turned over to Napoleon I of France.

Among other innovations, the newcomers introduced methods for producing more marketable crops. Coffee, brought to the island in 1736, became an important export by 1776, and sugarcane, which until then had been produced there only in small amounts, was augmented by large plantations using African slaves.

From 1765 to 1800 the slave population increased from about 5,000 to more than 13,300, although the proportion of slaves to the total population decreased because of the large influx of European colonists.

Spain's improved relations with Puerto Rico paid off militarily as the century ended. The British erroneously considered the island a weak link in the Spanish chain of imperial defenses because it had been a refuge for runaway slaves and a focus of clandestine trade and buccaneering operations.

In 1797 the British general Sir Ralph Abercromby led a naval force that captured Trinidad, which had been a somewhat neglected Spanish possession off the Venezuelan coast; however, Abercromby was firmly repulsed when he attacked Puerto Rico afterward.

In 1808, when Napoleon I invaded the Iberian Peninsula and placed his brother Joseph Bonaparte on the Spanish throne, the colonies of South and Central

America asserted their right to govern themselves in the name of the imprisoned Bourbon king, Ferdinand VII.

This claim to temporary self-rule evolved into a revolutionary movement for independence in most of the region; however, in Puerto Rico a different sequence of events ensued for various reasons.

All but one of the island's head districts offered little objection to Spain's strict mercantilist policies, which for many decades had ceased to affect their livelihoods.

In addition, most of the residents of San Juan remained dependent on Spain's administrative and military assistance and willingly followed imperial commands, though they ultimately served French designs.

As the revolutions progressed on the mainland, many loyal Spanish colonists found refuge in Puerto Rico rather than returning across the Atlantic to Europe. In 1815 the restored Bourbon government of Spain granted ample economic liberties to Puerto Ricans to reward their past loyalty and to ensure their future support for the empire.

The new reforms opened the island's ports to trade with foreign merchants, permitted the immigration of all Roman Catholics, regardless of nationality, and granted free land to the new settlers. The diverse immigrants contributed substantially to Puerto Rico's economic development.

Economic and political shifts

After 1830 Puerto Rico gradually developed a plantation economy based on sugarcane and coffee. Sugar and molasses, primarily exported to the United States, provided an important source of income for the Spanish government.

By the 1890s the population had reached nearly one million, and the value of foreign trade had increased considerably. Coffee exports provided the principal source of income, and the land area devoted to sugarcane was slowly expanding.

Political events during the 19th century were characterized by alternating periods of liberal reforms and conservative reactions, in part caused by the changes occurring in the Spanish government and Spain's antiquated system of colonial administration.

Puerto Ricans experienced two short periods of relative political freedom, 1809–14 and 1820–23, when the island was officially treated as an integral part of Spain with the right to elect representatives to the Spanish Cortes, or parliament.

Ramón Power y Giralt, who was selected to represent the island during the first period, succeeded in having the Cortes revoke the absolute powers of the island's colonial governor.

In the last period, Demetrio O'Daly convinced the Cortes to annul the colonial governor's control of the island's armed forces and permit freedom of the press.

However, in 1814 and again in 1820 the Spanish government curtailed these periods of moderate colonial rule and reinstated its absolutist control.

In 1837 a permanent constitutional monarchy was established in Spain; however, Spanish lawmakers argued that the colonies were not true Spanish provinces and therefore should be governed by special laws.

For more than three decades Puerto Ricans waited for the authoritarian rule of military colonial governors to loosen.

During that period political thought on the island began to crystallize, and requests were made for assimilation into the Spanish government and representation in the Cortes.

In contrast, a conservative bloc strongly favored the status quo, and a small third group advocated complete independence.

Movements Toward Self-government

A local commission, elected in 1865 to recommend governmental reforms, reported that slavery should be abolished before any other meaningful reforms were attempted. Political conservatives in Spain and on the island were shocked by the report, and the alarmed colonial government took steps to curtail a supposedly growing rebellious sentiment.

Some of the more outspoken and respected islanders were arrested and sent to Spain for trial.

Thus provoked, a small group of pro-independence radicals attempted an uprising, now known as the Grito de Lares, "Cry of Lares", on September 23, 1868.

The poorly planned revolt was quickly suppressed, but it took place concurrently with Cuba's struggle for independence, and the two events prompted Spain to grant several important reforms to Puerto Rico over the next few years.

In addition, Spain's first republican government came to power, forced Queen Isabella II to abdicate, and pardoned all political prisoners in the colonies and the mother country. The Spanish republic soon abolished slavery and allowed Puerto Rico another period of constitutional government, 1870–74.

During the 1880s Román Baldorioty de Castro led a movement for political autonomy under Spanish rule, which gained momentum at the expense of calls for directly integrating Puerto Rico into the Spanish government.

In 1887 the liberal movement was denounced as disloyal and was violently suppressed; however, such treatment only solidified popular support for the movement, and in 1897 the Autonomy Party was formed in Puerto Rico through cooperation with the Liberal Party in Spain.

The new autonomous government was parliamentary in form but was overseen by the governor-general as a representative of the Spanish king, who remained empowered to disband the insular parliament and suspend civil rights under special circumstances. The two-chamber parliament was responsible for local legislation, tariffs, and taxes.

The Spanish-American War

The brief Spanish-American War in 1898, which permitted the United States to take Cuba, Puerto Rico, the Philippines, and other colonial possessions from Spain, also effectively prevented Puerto Ricans from putting into effect their new government.

In May a U.S. naval force led by Adm. W.T. Sampson bombarded San Juan for a short time without serious casualties. On July 25 Gen. Nelson A. Miles landed a U.S. force of about 3,500 men at Guánica, on the south coast. He was met with only token military resistance and generally popular acceptance. Hostilities were ended on August 12 after a short campaign.

The United States viewed Puerto Rico as a profitable site for tropical agriculture, but its main purpose in seizing the island was to have a secure coaling station for its warships. This would guarantee a strong U.S. naval presence in the Caribbean and create a steppingstone toward the Isthmus of Panama, where a transoceanic canal would soon be built.

Rule by the United States

On October 18, 1898, Gen. John R. Brooke became military governor of Puerto Rico. Spain subsequently ceded the island to the United States by the Treaty of Paris, which was signed in December 1898 and ratified by the U.S. Senate in February 1899.

The military administration, which lasted until May 1900, successfully policed the island, established a public school system, managed government finances, and built sanitation networks, highways, and other public works. However, the military ruled with little regard for political or cultural sensitivities.

The U.S. Congress instituted civil government in Puerto Rico with the Foraker Act, May 1900, under which the United States continued to exercise the controlling power, a condition that proved distasteful to many Puerto Ricans; therefore, the law was subsequently amended to give Puerto Ricans a wider role in the government.

The Olmsted Act, approved by the U.S. Congress in July 1909, gave the U.S. president a more direct role in Puerto Rican affairs. However, the majority of Puerto Ricans eventually demanded a larger measure of local control and many other changes.

During World War I the U.S. Congress responded to these pressures and to the threat of German submarines prowling Caribbean waters by passing the Jones Act, which came into effect in March 1917.

Under its terms U.S. citizenship was conferred collectively on Puerto Ricans. However, the act failed to grant the measure of self-determination that Puerto Ricans had demanded considering the democratic tradition of the United States, because key officials, including the governor, remained presidential appointees and were thus beyond local control.

Despite the legal limitations on political autonomy, Puerto Ricans slowly developed a sense of greater liberty because of the change of sovereignty. At first this new order was sometimes mistrusted, resented, and misunderstood, but in the long run it was recognized as beneficial.

The powers of church and state were separated, resulting in open competition for religious adherence, and government programs began to deal directly with the vital needs of the people, including education, health and sanitation, and the regulation of working conditions, changes designed to remedy centuries of neglect.

Socioeconomic concerns

Early U.S. governors were mainly preoccupied with "Americanizing" Puerto Rican institutions, language, and political habits, but they had no clear policy regarding the island's eventual political status.

This lack of vision created strong resistance from many native leaders led by Luis Muñoz Rivera, who had fought for autonomy under Spain. The island's economy was completely reoriented, creating rapid and profound changes in all aspects of life.

Puerto Rican agricultural products, particularly sugarcane, were included within U.S. tariff walls and had a ready market; by 1899 the United States was buying almost two-thirds of Puerto Rican sugar production.

Puerto Rico, aided by the adoption of U.S. currency and by financial reforms, soon received large amounts of investment capital that revolutionized sugarcane production.

Three-fourths of the population became directly or indirectly dependent on sugarcane as land under cultivation expanded sevenfold between 1899 and 1939, new disease-resistant plants were imported, new styles of corporate management were implemented, and transportation facilities and large and efficient sugarcane-grinding mills were built.

The population increased from about 950,000 in 1899 to more than 1,540,000 in 1930.

The new focus on large-scale production sharpened social and political tensions as wealth was concentrated into fewer hands and formerly independent farmers lost their lands and became plantation employees.

In addition, the island was forced to import much of its food, and the government focused most of its aid on disaster relief and transportation problems rather than helping small-scale coffee growers.

Tobacco production increased until about 1930, when most smokers in the United States shifted from cigars to cigarettes, which are produced from a different type of tobacco plant.

In adding up to these economic changes, Puerto Ricans underwent a radical social change as modern sanitation practices and medical knowledge were applied to combat the island's high death rate.

The population seemed likely to double within two generations. The worldwide Great Depression struck during these changes, and U.S. government officials refocused their attention elsewhere. Recurring hurricanes and declining exports aggravated the economic distress of the island.

Political Developments

Most Puerto Rican political parties since 1898 had attempted to modify the political relations between the island and the U.S. federal government; the island's Republican Party favored statehood, whereas the Union Party worked for greater autonomy.

The Nationalist Party arose in the 1920s and argued for immediate independence. Meanwhile, the pro-U.S. Socialist Party, led by the highly respected labor leader Santiago Iglesias, remained focused on the plight of Puerto Rico's laboring classes, but its program had little support, because popular attention was largely concentrated on the political status of the island.

Puerto Rico was aided somewhat in the mid-1930s by Pres. Franklin D. Roosevelt's New Deal policies, which radically enlarged the previously accepted role of the government.

The newly formed Puerto Rican Reconstruction Administration, PRRA, attempted to redistribute economic power on the island, primarily by placing a restrictive quota on sugarcane production and enforcing a long-neglected law that limited corporate holdings to 500 acres, 200 hectares.

Thus, the PRRA reversed the growth of the island's sugarcane industry, and many Puerto Ricans sought to return to their small farms. The program provoked open opposition by the sugarcane companies, which were strongly represented in the Republican Party, but the Socialists tacitly accepted the program.

The strongest local proponent of the economic reforms was Luis Muñoz Marín, son of Luis Muñoz Rivera, who led a group of young radicals.

Two unconnected factors jeopardized the success of the New Deal program. First, the PRRA objectives were curtailed by administrative and financial problems, and the agency was unable to readjust completely the island's economic structure.

The second factor was related to a rise in violence by the Nationalists: the U.S. government, to counter the damage caused by the Nationalists, interjected the Puerto Rican status on the political scene.

The offer of independence, made when the island was facing adverse economic conditions, served to realign the political parties into pro-

and anti-independence groups and again distracted them from pressing economic issues.

Prior to the election of 1940, attention was again focused on the economy, and Muñoz Marín helped form a new party, the Popular Democratic Party (Partido Popular Democratic; PPD, to promote it as an issue.

The PPD aimed to improve the conditions of the lower classes, particularly the hardworking jíbaros of the mountainous interior, under the slogan "Bread, land, and liberty." A large part of the electorate supported the PPD, which gained tenuous control over the legislature.

The colonial governor, Rexford Guy Tug well, allowed the PPD to initiate such economic reforms as redistributing land, enforcing labor laws notably those regarding minimum wages and maximum hours, instituting a progressive income tax, and establishing an economic development program.

The PPD partially fulfilled its aims and was overwhelmingly backed by the electorate in 1944. Two years later U.S. Pres. Harry S. Truman appointed the island's first Puerto Rican governor, Jesús T. Piñero, and in 1947 the U.S. Congress allowed Puerto Rico to elect its governors by popular vote. Muñoz Marín was elected in November of the following year, and he took office in January 1949.

For more than a generation the PPD governed Puerto Rico, led mainly by Muñoz Marín during four terms as governor.

During the period 1948–68 Puerto Rico experienced a major economic change, shifting from agricultural dominance to an economy based on industrial production, largely through Operation Bootstrap, a government program that promoted economic development and social welfare.

The program initially promoted cooperative farming and labor-intensive industries, but when these efforts failed, the government invested heavily in transportation infrastructure and attracted privately owned factories through tax breaks and government-supported start-up costs.

These factors, together with low wages on the island, induced hundreds of U.S. and some European companies to open factories there. Workers increasingly left the sugarcane and coffee fields and moved into the coastal cities where wages, working conditions, and social services were improved. However, many also migrated to large metropolitan centers in the United States.

Chapter 17

The commonwealth of Puerto Rico

In addition to reforming the Puerto Rican economy, the PPD modified the island's political relationship with the United States. In October 1950 President Truman signed the Puerto Rico Commonwealth Bill, which enabled the island's people to establish their own constitution.

Some Puerto Ricans, notably the Nationalists, opposed the new law and resorted to violence. A handful of Nationalists unsuccessfully attempted to assassinate Gov. Muñoz Marín in San Juan, and Nationalist uprisings erupted in several island towns, causing 27 deaths. In November two New York-based Nationalists tried to kill Truman in Washington, D.C.

In 1951, Puerto Ricans overwhelmingly approved the commonwealth status in a referendum, and the island's constitution was proclaimed on July 25, 1952, a symbolic date because it was the 54th anniversary of the U.S. invasion of the island. The constitution reaffirmed the post of an elected governor, created a legislative branch in which minority representation was guaranteed, and set up a new judicial system based on civil liberties.

Dissatisfaction continued to be expressed despite broad popular support for the autonomy of the commonwealth government and a rapidly modernizing industrial society. Nationalist violence broke out again on March 1, 1954, in Washington, when four Nationalists, three men and a woman, fired weapons from the viewing galleries of the House of Representatives, wounding five Congressmen.

Legal reviews in the courts, both insular and federal, continued to enforce the commonwealth concept. At the same time, Puerto Ricans were unable to expand the limits of their autonomy to include international diplomacy, such as playing a greater role in Caribbean affairs. Sentiment in favor of statehood grew following the admission of Alaska and Hawaii to the United States, particularly because Puerto Ricans increasingly were depending on federal aid for the unemployed, elderly, and war veterans.

In addition, in 1959 Puerto Ricans became highly concerned over regional security and ideology following Fidel Castro's communist revolution in Cuba, and the island absorbed a sizable influx of Cuban exiles.

Muñoz Marín stepped down in 1964 and was succeeded by his able administrative assistant Roberto Sánchez Vilella, who in November of that year became the second elected governor in the island's history.

However, with the charismatic Muñoz Marín retired from the political scene, the PPD lost its firm grip on power and was fiercely opposed by pro-statehood groups.

In 1968 the PPD lost control of the lower house of the legislature after a split in its ranks, and it also relinquished the governorship to Luis A. Ferré, who led the pro-statehood New Progressive Party, Partido Nuevo Progresista; PNP. Since then, the PPD and PNP have alternated in power.

Puerto Rican society underwent sweeping changes during the 1960s and '70s. Agriculture lost importance, and there was rapid growth in manufacturing and in the number and size of urban and suburban settlements. In addition, cultural, political, and economic links with the United States increased as greater numbers of Puerto Ricans migrated there.

The U.S. government introduced food stamps in 1974 to improve the diets of poorer residents, and by 1980 about three-fifths of the population was receiving the benefit.

The PPD returned to power briefly in 1973–76 under the leadership of Rafael Hernández Colón, a young protégé of Muñoz Marín. The pro-statehood PNP regained power in 1976 under the vigorous leadership of Carlos Romero Barceló, but Hernández Colón won back the governorship for the PPD in 1984 and served for two terms.

In November 1992, Pedro Rossello, a medical doctor, led the pro-statehood PNP to another electoral victory, and he was reelected governor in 1996. However, a series of corruption scandals soon caused the PNP to lose support. In November 2000 the mayor of San Juan, Sila Calderón of the pro-commonwealth PPD, was elected as Puerto Rico's first woman governor.

The appointment of Sonia Sotomayor, a judge of Puerto Rican descent, to the U.S. Supreme Court in 2009 inspired pride that transcended political affiliation.

The debate Over Political Status

In 1952, after Puerto Rico was granted commonwealth status, the United States advised the United Nations, UN, that the island was a self-governing territory. However, dissatisfaction with the island's political status continued.

A commission appointed by the U.S. Congress concluded that three options, commonwealth, statehood, or independence, should be considered in a plebiscite, which was held in July 1967.

The majority PPD supported the plebiscite, but it was boycotted by the pro-statehood and independence parties. The result showed that 60.4 percent of the electorate supported commonwealth status, 38.9 percent statehood, and 0.6 percent independence.

Both the leaders of the PPD and influential members of the U.S. federal government agreed that the commonwealth relationship needed to be improved and the degree of self-government broadened.

However, no other action was taken, partly because political power on the island began to alternate between pro-commonwealth and pro-statehood parties.

After the pro-statehood PNP swept to victory in the 1992 gubernatorial elections, it pushed for a second plebiscite, which was held in November 1993 with nearly three-fourths of the 2.2 million eligible voters taking part; the pro-commonwealth option won by a plurality of 48.6 percent, followed by 46.3 percent for statehood and 4 percent for independence.

When the PNP governor won a second term in 1996, the party mounted a campaign to hold still another plebiscite; however, the PPD, protesting that the definition of commonwealth on the ballot was inadequate, urged its followers to vote for "none of the above."

In the December 1998 plebiscite, the "none of the above" option won most 50.3 percent of the vote, followed by 46.6 percent for statehood and 2.5 percent for independence, marking the third time in three decades that statehood had been rebuffed by Puerto Rican voters.

In July 1999 Gov. Pedro Rosselló urged the UN decolonization committee to intervene by putting Puerto Rico back on the list of non-self-governing territories. Until that time, only pro-independence groups had actively lobbied at the UN, decrying Puerto Rico's "colonial" status.

Now, pro-statehood activists were joining the effort, out of frustration with Washington's apparent reluctance to either embrace statehood or expand Puerto Rico's autonomous powers.

Washington policymakers, in turn, have highlighted the Puerto Ricans' inability to reach a consensus on political status. Several members of Congress have expressed doubts about the ability of the United States to absorb a Spanish-speaking state, while others have voiced concern that statehood would sharply increase the already large amount of federal funds flowing to the island.

The controversial issue of Vieques, an island municipality of Puerto Rico, has united Puerto Ricans across party lines. The U.S. Navy, which owns two-thirds of Vieques, began military maneuvers there, including bombing practice, in the mid-20th century. Opposition to the navy's use of the island intensified after two off-target bombs killed a civilian guard on the bombing range in 1999.

Protesters subsequently prevented the navy from carrying out many of its maneuvers on Vieques, and Puerto Rican officials of all three major parties cited health and environmental concerns as they lobbied for an end to military exercises there. In 2001 the U.S. government announced plans for a gradual cessation of the maneuvers.

Few Puerto Ricans consider political status to be one of the key problems facing the commonwealth, but the island's leaders continue to push for a resolution. Most of the people clearly value some form of permanent association with the United States, although Puerto Ricans fiercely embrace their language and Hispanic American culture; some have even pointed out that, under statehood, Puerto Rico could no longer field its own teams for the Olympic Games.

As the debate continued into the 21st century, striking parallels could be drawn to the period of Spanish colonial rule, when the choices of full assimilation, statehood, autonomy, commonwealth, or independence for the island were also deliberated.

On November 2012 Puerto Ricans went to the polls for the fourth time in 45 years to attempt to settle the question of the commonwealth's political status.

The two-part nonbinding referendum asked voters if they felt Puerto Rico should continue under its present form of territorial status. Some 54 percent of those who voted indicated that they were not satisfied with that status.

The second part of the referendum asked voters if they wanted the island to become a U.S. state, an independent country, or a "sovereign free-associated state." About 61 percent of those who voted chose statehood; however, hundreds of thousands of voters left the question blank, presumably because they had not been offered other non-statehood options, including the possibility of remaining a commonwealth.

In the eyes of many U.S. lawmakers, those limited choices brought into question whether a majority of Puerto Ricans wanted statehood.

The island's political status was a pivotal element in the financial crisis that reached a crescendo at the end of June 2015, when Gov. Alejandro García Padilla announced that Puerto Rico could no longer meet its debt obligations. Although not a U.S. state,

Puerto Rico was treated like a state and not a municipality under the U.S. federal bankruptcy code and therefore could not declare bankruptcy. Repeated attempts to balance Puerto Rico's budget through austerity measures, tax increases, and further borrowing had failed to arrest its debt spiral, and García Padilla called on creditors to restructure his government's debt and beseeched the federal government to make it possible for the commonwealth to declare bankruptcy.

Because Puerto Rican bonds were widely held and were common elements of many mutual funds the potential ripple impact of the crisis on the U.S. economy was significant.

At the end of June 2016, U.S. Pres. Barack Obama signed into law the Puerto Rico Oversight, Management and Economic Stability Act PROMESA, which authorized the Puerto Rican government to restructure more than $70 billion in debt.

The act also created a federally appointed seven-member oversight board to control Puerto Rico's finances, a stipulation that was only grudgingly accepted by García Padilla, who chose not to run for reelection. In November Ricardo Rosselló, a pro-statehood candidate, was elected to succeed García Padilla.

On September 20, 2017, Puerto Rico was hammered by Hurricane Maria, a near category 5 cyclone that produced winds of up to 155 miles 250 km per hour and dropped some 30 inches 750 mm of rain on parts of the island in just one day.

The devastation produced by the storm was massive; the damage was estimated at more than $90 billion. Much of Puerto Rico's outdated electricity infrastructure was destroyed; as late as nearly five months after the storm, some 400,000 of the island's electricity customers still were without power.

The official count of deaths that resulted from the disaster was 64, but some estimates attributed more than 1,000 deaths to the storm. In August 2018 the commonwealth government raised the official death toll to nearly 3,000.

That figure was based on the results of a study that the government had commissioned from the Milken Institute School of Public Health at the George Washington University, which concluded that the initial official count had considered only those who were killed directly by the hurricane through drowning or injury by collapsed buildings or flying wreckage and failed to take into account the fatalities resulting from the long-term, six-month, consequences of the disaster.

On September 18, 2022, Puerto Rico was again hit by a hurricane. Although not as strong as Maria, Hurricane Fiona caused flooding and landslides, and it knocked out the island's electricity.

Culebra Island, Spanish Isla De Culebra, island, Puerto Rico, 20 miles, 30 km, east of Puerto Rico Island and 15 miles west of St. Thomas, Virgin Islands. The island fronts north on the Atlantic Ocean and south and west on Vieques Sound, which connects the Atlantic with the Caribbean Sea. About 7 miles, 11 km, long and 2 miles 3 km wide, Culebra Island is 10 square miles, 26 square km, in area.

Its hilly, almost barren mass of limestone and igneous intrusions rises to 646 feet, 197 meters, at Mount Resaca.

The island's deep bay, Puerto Grande, on the southeast, was used as a U.S. naval base until 1975. Culebra has sparse, thin soils and no permanent streams; tourism and fishing are the principal activities of its few inhabitants.

Armed Forces and Police

Puerto Rico continues to be a strategic site for the U.S. military. For decades the U.S. Navy has occupied a large base at Roosevelt Roads, on the east coast.

By 2001 local protests had mounted against the navy's use of a portion of the nearby island of Vieques for its maneuvers, including gunnery and bombing practice, and the federal government, bowing to public pressure, announced plans to halt the bombing.

Drug interdiction in Puerto Rico

Unlike the various municipal, county, and state police forces common in the United States, Puerto Rico has a single, centralized police force, which includes a body of detectives. Puerto Rico is considered a major transshipment point for illegal drugs from South America to North America, and local and U.S. law enforcement agencies have long been engaged in drug interdiction efforts there.

Education

More than nine-tenths of the people are literate. Schooling is compulsory and free for children between the ages of 6 and 16. Although most children complete at least eight years of education, there is a high dropout rate.

About half of Puerto Ricans, age 25 and older are high school graduates, and bachelor's degrees are held by one-seventh of the population nearly one-fourth of high school graduates. Puerto Rico invests heavily in education nearly one-third of its annual budget—notably in vocational and technical programs, and U.S. federal funds also encourage attendance in schools and universities. The main public institution of higher learning is the University of Puerto Rico founded in 1903, with its main campus at Río Piedras.

Among the several private universities and colleges are the Inter-American University, 1912, which has several campuses, and the Pontifical Catholic University 1948 in Ponce.

Health and Welfare

In 1947 the Puerto Rican birth rate was about 43 per 1,000 people, whereas life expectancy at birth was only about 50 years. Health conditions subsequently improved dramatically, approaching the standards of the U.S. states. The life expectancy at birth is now some 79 years for Puerto Rican women and 71 for men.

Major causes of death include heart disease, cancers, diabetes, cerebrovascular diseases, and pneumonia and influenza. Urban clinics and rural health centers provide basic medical care, and the U.S. Medicare and Medicaid programs have contributed to improving health among lower-income residents, as have various other social programs.

In the 1990s the Puerto Rican government initiated financial reforms of the health care system, including privatizing some hospitals and clinics.

The government has long worked to upgrade rural and urban areas with piped water, electricity, and other amenities. It has also improved the housing situation, notably through its Urban Renewal and Housing Corporation, which concentrates on low-income housing projects. A water-treatment system and aqueduct, laid out along the coast from north-central Puerto Rico to San Juan, opened in 2000.

Cultural Life

The idealized folk hero of Puerto Rico is the jíbaro, a rustic independent hill-farmer whose status in local song and story is like that of the gaucho of Argentina. However, modern Puerto Rican cultural life is a blend of North American and Latin, African, and Caribbean forms, as is evident in much of the island's dance, music, art, literature, and sports.

The pre-Columbian Taino culture, which was largely decimated by European colonizers, has had only limited impact on Puerto Rican life and is evident mainly in the use of certain linguistic expressions and words incorporated into the Spanish language, such as hamaca "hammock", cacique "chief", and tabaco "tobacco".

African influences are found in food, music, and art. Music festivals, museums in Ponce and San Juan, and theatrical performances encourage Hispanidad, or Spanish customs. Puerto Ricans have worked to preserve a Latin heritage while welcoming U.S. economic and social novelties, engendering a cultural dilemma that has often catalyzed political debate.

Daily Life

Puerto Rican lifestyles have changed rapidly as new technologies, economic opportunities, and patterns of development emerged. The island remains far poorer than the United States, but its growing middle class has adopted living standards that would be familiar to most North Americans.

Some two-thirds of Puerto Rican families own their own homes. Large expanses of former farmland have been converted to suburban communities, urbanizations, rural wooden shacks have been replaced by sturdy cement houses equipped with modern appliances, and cars have increasingly clogged modern highways, particularly during evening rush hours in the San Juan area.

A voracious appetite for consumer goods, coupled with easy access to credit, prompts shoppers to jam air-conditioned suburban malls that feature U.S. chain stores, fast-food restaurants, and multiplex cinemas.

On most Saturday nights in San Juan, well-dressed young suburbanites crowd the dance floors of nightclubs and hotels, once the exclusive province of tourists or frequent the bars and cafés of historic Old San Juan.

Puerto Ricans continue to prefer traditional dishes with rice and beans, plantains, and beef, chicken, or pork. However, North American fast-food restaurants that sell hamburgers, pizza, and other fare are growing in popularity, particularly among the young.

Traditional Creole foods include sopa de arroz con pollo, chicken-and-rice soup), sancocho, a beef-and-vegetable stew, tostones, fried plantain slices, flan, and casabe, powdery cakes made from ground cassava, often served with molasses and coconut milk.

Local supermarkets are well stocked with traditional fare as well as frozen and processed foods, which are mainly imported from the United States. Locally produced soft drinks and rums are also popular.

Cultural Institutions

Most of Puerto Rico's cultural institutions, including its major universities and libraries, are concentrated in the San Juan area. The Puerto Rican Athenium, Ateneo Puertorriqueño; 1876, is a prestigious learned society.

The University of Puerto Rico Library System, 1903, is the island's main library, with more than four million holdings divided among 12 sites. Works by Puerto Rican painters and sculptors are displayed in the Museum of Contemporary Art,

1984 and the Puerto Rican Museum of Art, 2000, which are in San Juan. Also notable are the Ponce Art Museum, 1959 and the Museum of Religious Art, the latter housed in a 17th-century church in San Germán.

The Luis A. Ferré Fine Arts Centre,1981) in San Juan is the venue for many theatrical and musical events. Among the island's research centers are the Institute of Puerto Rican Culture, 1955, and the International Institute of Tropical Forestry, 1939.

The Arecibo Observatory, 1963–2020, a radio telescope with a 1,000-foot, 305-metre diameter, was, for most of its life, the largest of its kind in the world. It collapsed in 2020.

Francisco Oller

Some of the island's earliest inhabitants created polychrome ceramics, amulets, and stone carvings. About 1000 CE the Taino used granite, marble, and other types of stone to carve three-pointed figures with human and animal features; they also produced ceremonial stools, wooden rattles, petroglyphs surrounding their ball courts, and stone-carved ceremonial belts or collars.

During Puerto Rico's colonial period, African slaves formed multicolored coconut-fibre masks for local festivals, a tradition that is still carried on. José de Rivafrecha y Campeche (1751–1809) was the island's first major painter. The most notable 19th-century painters were Ramón Atiles y Pérez and Francisco Oller. More recent artists include Julio Rosado del Valle, Rafael Tufiño, Antonio Martorell, and Augusto Marín.

Literature

Contemporary poets, novelists, short-story writers, and essayists keep alive the traditions of such 19th-century forerunners as novelist Manuel Zeno Gandía, playwright Alejandro Tapia, essayist Eugenio María de Hostos, and poet José Gautier Benítez.

Leading 20th-century and contemporary authors include novelists and short-story writers Abelardo Díaz Alfaro, Enrique Laguerre, Pedro Juan Soto, Emilio Díaz Valcárcel, José Luis González, and Rosario Ferré; poets Julia de Burgos and Luis Palés Matos whose works reflect Afro-Caribbean influences; playwright René Marqués; and poet and playwright Pedro Pietri, who inspired young Puerto Ricans living in New

York City, called Nuyoricans, by composing poetry that instilled pride in their culture and heritage.

Performing arts

Puerto Rican musicians, composers, and actors have made marks far beyond their island's shores, and some have been counted among the world's most famous pop-culture figures. Notable Puerto Rican stage and screen performers included the Academy Award winners José Ferrer, Rita Moreno, and Benicio Del Toro, as well as Raúl Juliá. Other performers of Puerto Rican descent included Chita Rivera and Jennifer Lopez.

Among 19th-century composers are Manuel Tavárez and Juan Morel Campos, both known for their dance melodies. The popular 20th-century songwriter Rafael Hernández is still revered throughout Latin America.

The Spanish-born cellist Pablo Casals, whose mother was Puerto Rican, moved to the island in 1956 and founded the world-famous classical music festival there that bears his name. Puerto Rican musicians have included the classical pianist Jesus María Sanromá, opera singers Antonio Paoli and Justino Díaz, and popular musicians Ruth Fernández, Tito Puente, José Feliciano, Cheo Feliciano, Ricky Martin, and Calle 13.

Latin jazz and salsa are enjoyed throughout the island; also popular are merengue, rock, rap, the Afro-Caribbean bomba, and the tambourine-marked plena. Many musical groups preserve jíbaro, folk, music by playing such instruments as the cuatro, a small guitar carved from a single piece of wood, the marímbula, a wooden box on which are mounted tuned metal tongues, the güiro, a percussive gourd that is also a popular decoration, drums, and maracas.

Sports and Recreation

Baseball is Puerto Rico's national sport, and the island has long been a source for U.S. major-league players, including Roberto Clemente,

Orlando Cepeda, Juan "Igor" González, Bernie Williams, Roberto Hernández, Iván Rodríguez, and Leo Gómez. Boxing and basketball are also popular. Puerto Rican boxers of note include José Torres, Edwin Rosario, Hector Camacho, and Félix "Tito" Trinidad. Cockfighting and Thoroughbred horse racing events (where gambling is permitted) are also well attended. Puerto Rico has competed in the Olympic Games since 1948, and its boxers are frequent contenders for medals.

Puerto Rico observes many of the secular holidays of the United States, and, as elsewhere in Latin America, its municipalities celebrate numerous religious festivals centered on the feast days of patron saints.

The Festival of St. John the Baptist, June 24, in San Juan climaxes at midnight when revelers walk backward into the sea, an act said to bring good luck. Ponce hosts a pre-Lenten Carnival featuring horn-masked celebrants who dance and take part in parades, and the town of Hatillo holds the Carnival-like Festival of the Masks each December 28.

Press and Broadcasting

The commonwealth has a free press, and local and major U.S. newspapers are widely available, as are foreign publications. Puerto Rico has several weekly and daily periodicals, the largest of which are El Nuevo Día, El Vocero de Puerto Rico, and the San Juan Star, which has both English- and Spanish-language editions.

The first radio broadcast in Puerto Rico was made in 1923, and the island now has some 120 AM and FM radio stations—giving it one of the world's highest densities of radio broadcasters. Nearly all broadcasts are in Spanish. Television was introduced in 1954, and there are now a dozen Spanish-language TV stations, with programming comparable to that shown in the United States. Puerto Rico also has government radio and television stations, which feature educational and cultural broadcasts. English-language channels and other programming are available via cable television and satellite.

Chapter 18

European Settlement

The following discussion focuses on Puerto Rican history from the time of European settlement. For treatment of the island in its regional context, see Latin America, history of, and West Indies, history of sculpture of Taino Indians.

The first inhabitants of Puerto Rico were hunter-gatherers who reached the island more than 1,000 years before the arrival of the Spanish. Arawak Indians, who developed the Taino culture, had also settled there by 1000 CE. The clan-based Taino lived in small villages led by a cacique, or chief.

They had a limited knowledge of agriculture but grew such domesticated tropical crops as pineapples, cassava, and sweet potatoes and supplemented their diet with seafood. In the late 15th century 20,000–50,000 Taino lived on Puerto Rico, which they called Borinquen, Borinquén, or Boriken.

The Taino occasionally warded off attacks by their Carib neighbors from islands to the south and east, including the Virgin Islands and Vieques Island.

In 1493 Christopher Columbus left Spain on his second voyage to the Indies with a large expedition of 17 ships and about 1,500 men. At the island of Guadeloupe, the Spaniards rescued several Taino prisoners whom the Carib had taken from Borinquen, and Columbus agreed to return them to their island.

On November 19, 1493, Columbus anchored in a bay on the west coast of Borinquen, which he promptly renamed San Juan Bautista "Saint John the Baptist" and claimed for the Spanish monarchs Ferdinand II and Isabella I. The expeditionary spent two days on the island before sailing westward to Hispaniola, where they established the first permanent settlement in the New World.

Early Settlement

For 15 years San Juan Bautista was neglected except for an occasional visit by a ship putting in for supplies. In 1508 Juan Ponce de León, who had accompanied Columbus and worked to colonize Hispaniola, was granted permission to explore the island.

On the north coast Ponce de León found an exceptionally well-protected bay that could harbor a large number of sailing vessels; on high ground beside the bay, he founded Caparra, the island's first town and the site of its first mining and agricultural operations. By 1521 the town was moved to an islet at the northern end of the harbor and renamed Puerto Rico, "Rich Port".

Through time and common usage, the port became known as San Juan while the name Puerto Rico came to be applied to the whole island.

The Taino soon lost admiration for their Spanish "protectors," who expected the Indians to act as slaves, paying tribute in gold and food as well as accepting instruction in the Christian religion.

Meanwhile, European diseases to which the Spaniards were largely immune, and maltreatment had begun to destroy the Taino population.

In 1511, the Indians rebelled but had only temporary success against the better-armed Spanish, who again subjugated them. The Spanish subsequently brought Indian slaves from nearby islands and black slaves from Africa to fully staff their placer mines.

However, gold production markedly declined after the 1530s, and many of the Europeans migrated elsewhere.

Those who remained set up sugarcane and ginger plantations with their African slaves, but the colony continued to lead a precarious existence. Carib groups from neighboring islands made frequent raids, carrying off food and slaves and destroying property.

Puerto Rico was further destroyed by disease, and it was robbed by French, British, and Dutch pirates.

During the mid-16th century French forces repeatedly burned and destroyed San Germán, the island's second settlement. Increasing numbers of colonists left the island.

San Cristóbal fortress, San Juan, Puerto Rico

In the second half of the 16th century Spain, recognizing the strategic importance of Puerto Rico, undertook to convert San Juan into a military outpost by using a financial subsidy from the Mexican mines.

Initially they built a fortified palace for the governor called La Fortaleza, "The Fortress", followed by the massive San Felipe del Morro (El Morro) castle, which was perfectly located to dominate the narrow entrance to the harbor.

Finally, they added a stronger and larger fortress, San Cristóbal, to the northeast, on the Atlantic side of the city. In the early 17th century, the city was surrounded by a stone wall 25 feet,8 meters, high and 18 feet, 5 meters, thick, two parts of which still stand. These defenses made San Juan almost impregnable.

San Juan: El Morro

In 1595 Sir Francis Drake attacked the city with a sizable fleet but failed to silence its guns. Three years later the British soldier George Clifford, 3rd earl of Cumberland, captured the city but was soon forced to abandon it after his troops fell victim to disease.

In 1625, the Dutchman Bowdoin Hendrik captured and burned the town but failed to subdue El Morro, where the governor had taken refuge.

San Juan, the most exposed military outpost guarding Spain's New World empire, received political and economic attention from the mother country; however, the island's rural inhabitants, or jíbaros, were typically ignored by Spain and despised by the residents of San Juan.

The jíbaros thus resisted for themselves and cultivated their own small landholdings. As the French, British, Danish, and Dutch fought over and settled the Lesser Antilles during the 17th and 18th centuries, the colonial authorities of San Juan rarely ventured beyond their walled defenses for fear of buccaneer attacks.

The jíbaros, ignoring the laws of Spain, prospered somewhat by trading clandestinely with non-Spanish merchants. Ginger, hides, sugarcane, tobacco, and cattle from the island were in great demand.

The settlers' contact with foreigners did not turn them away from their mother country, as the Spanish crown had feared, instead, they remained loyal and willing to participate in military expeditions.

Chapter 19

Liberal reforms and regional turmoil

During the 18th century, Spain's Bourbon rulers ordered their colonial representatives to carry out sweeping economic and administrative reforms that promoted trade between Puerto Rico and Spain, stimulated agricultural production.

They integrated the island's various military units into a unified command. All in order they converted Puerto Rico from a financial drain to a major economic asset.

The enlightened dictatorship of the Spanish Bourbons encouraged Puerto Rico's commercial agriculture. The island's population grew rapidly, from roughly 45,000 in 1765 to more than 103,000 in 1787 and 155,000 in 1800.

By the end of the 18th century there were 34 towns on the island. Among the larger immigrant groups were Canary Islanders, French settlers from Louisiana or Haiti, and Spaniards from Santo Domingo, later the Dominican Republic. It had been turned over to Napoleon I of France.

Among other innovations, the newcomers introduced methods for producing more marketable crops. Coffee, brought to the island in 1736, became an important export by 1776, and sugarcane, which until then had been produced there only in small amounts, was augmented by large plantations using African slaves.

From 1765 to 1800 the slave population increased from about 5,000 to more than 13,300, although the proportion of slaves to the total population decreased because of the large influx of European colonists.

Spain's improved relations with Puerto Rico paid off militarily as the century drew to a close. The British erroneously considered the island a weak link in the Spanish chain of imperial defenses because it had been a refuge for runaway slaves and a focus of clandestine trade and buccaneering operations.

In 1797 the British general Sir Ralph Abercromby led a naval force that captured Trinidad, which had been a somewhat neglected Spanish possession off the Venezuelan coast; however, Abercromby was firmly repulsed when he attacked Puerto Rico afterward.

In 1808, when Napoleon I invaded the Iberian Peninsula and placed his brother Joseph Bonaparte on the Spanish throne, the colonies of South and Central America asserted their right to govern themselves in the name of the imprisoned Bourbon king, Ferdinand VII.

This claim to temporary self-rule evolved into a revolutionary movement for independence in most of the region; however, in Puerto Rico a different sequence of events ensued for various reasons.

All but one of the island's head districts offered little objection to Spain's strict mercantilist policies, which for many decades had ceased to affect their livelihoods. In addition, most of the residents of San Juan remained dependent on Spain's administrative and military assistance and willingly followed imperial commands, though they ultimately served French designs.

As the revolutions progressed on the mainland, many loyal Spanish colonists found refuge in Puerto Rico rather than returning across the Atlantic to Europe. In 1815 the restored Bourbon government of Spain granted ample economic liberties to Puerto Ricans in an attempt to reward their past loyalty and to ensure their future support for the empire.

The new reforms opened the island's ports to trade with foreign merchants, permitted the immigration of all Roman Catholics, regardless of nationality, and granted free land to the new settlers. The diverse immigrants contributed substantially to Puerto Rico's economic development.

Economic and Political Shifts

After 1830, Puerto Rico gradually developed a plantation economy based on sugarcane and coffee. Sugar and molasses, primarily exported to the United States, provided an important source of income for the Spanish government.

By the 1890s the population had reached nearly one million, and the value of foreign trade had increased considerably. Coffee exports provided the principal source of income, and the land area devoted to sugarcane was slowly expanding.

Political events during the 19th century were characterized by alternating periods of liberal reforms and conservative reactions, in part caused by the changes occurring in the Spanish government and Spain's antiquated system of colonial administration.

Puerto Ricans experienced two short periods of relative political freedom, 1809–14 and 1820–23, when the island was officially treated as an integral part of Spain with the right to elect representatives to the Spanish Cortes, or parliament.

Ramón Power y Giralt, who was selected to represent the island during the first period, succeeded in having the Cortes revoke the absolute powers of the island's colonial governor. In the latter period Demetrio O'Daly convinced the

Cortes to annul the colonial governor's control of the island's armed forces and permit freedom of the press. However, in 1814 and again in 1820 the Spanish government curtailed these periods of moderate colonial rule and reinstated its absolutist control.

In 1837, a permanent constitutional monarchy was established in Spain; however, Spanish lawmakers argued that the colonies were not true Spanish provinces and therefore should be governed by special laws.

For more than three decades Puerto Ricans waited for the despotic rule of military colonial governors to loosen. During that period political thought on the island began to crystallize, and requests were made for assimilation into the Spanish government and representation in the Cortes. In contrast, a conservative bloc strongly favored the status quo, and a small third group advocated complete independence.

Movements Toward Self-government

A local commission, elected in 1865, to recommend governmental reforms, reported that slavery should be abolished before any other meaningful reforms were attempted.

Political conservatives in Spain and on the island were shocked by the report, and the alarmed colonial government took steps to curtail a supposedly growing rebellious sentiment. Some of the more outspoken and respected islanders were arrested and sent to Spain for trial.

Thus provoked, a small group of pro-independence radicals attempted an uprising, now known as the Grito de Lares, "Cry of Lares", on September 23, 1868.

The poorly planned revolt was quickly suppressed, but it took place concurrently with Cuba's struggle for independence, and the two events prompted Spain to grant several important reforms to Puerto Rico over the next few years.

In addition, Spain's first republican government came to power, forced Queen.

Isabella II to abdicate and pardoned all political prisoners in the colonies and the mother country. The Spanish republic soon abolished slavery and allowed Puerto Rico another period of constitutional government, 1870–74.

During the 1880s Román Baldorioty de Castro led a movement for political autonomy under Spanish rule, which gained momentum at the expense of calls for directly integrating Puerto Rico into the Spanish government.

In 1887 the liberal movement was denounced as disloyal and was violently suppressed; however, such treatment only solidified popular support for the movement, and in 1897 the Autonomy Party was formed in Puerto Rico through cooperation with the Liberal Party in Spain.

The new autonomous government was parliamentary in form but was overseen by the governor-general as a representative of the Spanish king, who remained empowered to disband the insular parliament and suspend civil rights under special circumstances. The two-chamber parliament was responsible for local legislation, tariffs, and taxes.

Chapter 20

The Spanish-American War

The brief Spanish-American War, 1898, which permitted the United States to take Cuba, Puerto Rico, the Philippines, and other colonial possessions from Spain, also effectively prevented Puerto Ricans from putting into effect their new government. In May a U.S. naval force led by Adm. W.T. Sampson bombarded San Juan for a short time without serious casualties.

On July 25, Gen. Nelson A. Miles landed a U.S. force of about 3,500 men at Guánica, on the south coast. He was met with only token military resistance and generally popular acceptance. Hostilities were ended on August 12 after a short campaign.

The United States viewed Puerto Rico as a profitable site for tropical agriculture, but its main purpose in seizing the island was to have a secure coaling station for its warships. This would guarantee a strong U.S. naval presence in the Caribbean and create a steppingstone toward the Isthmus of Panama, where a transoceanic canal would soon be built.

Rule by the United States

On October 18, 1898, Gen. John R. Brooke became military governor of Puerto Rico. Spain subsequently surrendered the island to the United States by the Treaty of Paris, which was signed in December 1898 and ratified by the U.S. Senate in February 1899.

The military administration, which lasted until May 1900, successfully policed the island, established a public school system, managed government finances, and built sanitation networks, highways, and other public works.

The military ruled with little regard for political or cultural sensitivities. The U.S. Congress instituted civil government in Puerto Rico with the Foraker Act (May 1900), under which the United States continued to exercise the controlling power, a condition that proved distasteful to many Puerto Ricans; therefore, the law was subsequently amended to give Puerto Ricans a wider role in the government.

The Olmsted Act, approved by the U.S. Congress in July 1909, gave the U.S. president a more direct role in Puerto Rican affairs. The majority of Puerto Ricans eventually demanded a larger measure of local control and many other changes.

During World War I the U.S. Congress responded to these pressures and to the threat of German submarines prowling Caribbean waters by passing the Jones Act, which came into effect in March 1917.

Under its terms U.S. citizenship was conferred collectively on Puerto Ricans. However, the act failed to grant the measure of self-determination that Puerto Ricans had demanded considering the democratic tradition of the United States, because key officials, including the governor, remained presidential appointees and were thus beyond local control.

Despite the legal limitations on political autonomy, Puerto Ricans slowly developed a sense of greater liberty because of the change of sovereignty. At first this new order was sometimes mistrusted, resented, and misunderstood, but in the long run it was recognized as beneficial.

The powers of church and state were separated, resulting in open competition for religious adherence, and government programs began to deal directly with the vital needs of the people, including education, health and sanitation, and the regulation of working conditions— changes designed to remedy centuries of neglect.

Luis Muñoz Rivera

Early U.S. governors were mainly preoccupied with "Americanizing" Puerto Rican institutions, language, and political habits, but they had no clear policy regarding the island's eventual political status.

This lack of vision created strong resistance from many native leaders led by Luis Muñoz Rivera, who had fought for autonomy under Spain. The island's economy was completely reoriented, creating rapid and profound changes in all aspects of life.

Puerto Rican agricultural products, particularly sugarcane, were included within U.S. tariff walls and had a ready market; by 1899 the United States was buying almost two-thirds of Puerto Rican sugar production. Puerto Rico, aided by the adoption of U.S. currency and by financial reforms, soon received large amounts of investment capital that revolutionized sugarcane production.

Three-fourths of the population became directly or indirectly dependent on sugarcane as land under cultivation expanded sevenfold between 1899 and 1939, new disease-resistant plants were imported, new styles of corporate management were implemented, and transportation facilities and large and efficient sugarcane-grinding mills were built.

The population increased from about 950,000 in 1899 to more than 1,540,000 in 1930....

The new focus on large-scale production sharpened social and political tensions as wealth was concentrated into fewer hands and formerly independent farmers lost their lands and became plantation employees.

In addition, the island was forced to import much of its food, and the government focused most of its aid on disaster relief and transportation problems rather than helping small-scale coffee growers.

Tobacco production increased until about 1930, when most smokers in the United States shifted from cigars to cigarettes, which are produced from a different type of tobacco plant.

In addition to these economic changes, Puerto Ricans underwent a radical social change as modern sanitation practices and medical knowledge were applied to combat the island's high death rate.

The population seemed likely to double within two generations. The worldwide Great Depression struck during these changes, and U.S. government officials refocused their attention elsewhere. Recurring hurricanes and declining exports aggravated the economic distress of the island.

Political Developments

Most Puerto Rican political parties since 1898 had attempted to modify the political relations between the island and the U.S. federal government. The island's Republican Party favored statehood, whereas the Union Party worked for greater autonomy.

The Nationalist Party arose in the 1920s and argued for immediate independence. Meanwhile, the pro-U.S. Socialist Party, led by the highly respected labor leader Santiago Iglesias, remained focused on the plight of Puerto Rico's laboring classes, but its program had little support, because popular attention was largely concentrated on the political status of the island.

Puerto Rico was aided somewhat in the mid-1930s by Pres. Franklin D. Roosevelt's New Deal policies, which radically enlarged the previously accepted role of the government.

The newly formed Puerto Rican Reconstruction Administration, PRRA, attempted to redistribute economic power on the island, primarily by placing a restrictive quota on sugarcane production and enforcing a long-neglected law that limited corporate holdings to 500 acres.

Thus, the PRRA reversed the growth of the island's sugarcane industry, and many Puerto Ricans sought to return to their small farms. The program provoked open opposition by the sugarcane companies, which were strongly represented in the Republican Party, but the Socialists tacitly accepted the program. The strongest local proponent of the economic reforms was Luis Muñoz Marín, son of Luis Muñoz Rivera, who led a group of young radicals.

Luis Muñoz Marín

Two unconnected factors jeopardized the success of the New Deal program. First, the PRRA objectives were curtailed by administrative and financial problems, and the agency was unable to readjust completely the island's economic structure.

The second factor was related to a rise in violence by the Nationalists: the U.S. government, in order to counter the damage caused by the Nationalists, interjected the issue of Puerto Rican status on the political scene.

The offer of independence, made when the island was facing adverse economic conditions, served to realign the political parties into pro- and anti-independence groups and again distracted them from pressing economic issues.

Rexford Guy Tugwell

Prior to the election of 1940, attention was again focused on the economy, and Muñoz Marín helped form a new party, the Popular Democratic Party, Partido Popular Democratic; PPD, to promote it as an issue.

The PPD aimed to improve the conditions of the lower classes, particularly the hardworking jíbaros of the mountainous interior, under the slogan "Bread, land, and liberty."

A large part of the electorate supported the PPD, which gained tenuous control over the legislature. The colonial governor, Rexford Guy Tugwell, allowed the PPD to initiate such economic reforms as redistributing land, enforcing labor laws, notably those regarding minimum wages and maximum hours, instituting a progressive income tax, and establishing an economic development program.

The PPD partially fulfilled its aims and was overwhelmingly backed by the electorate in 1944.

Two years later U.S. Pres. Harry S. Truman appointed the island's first Puerto Rican governor, Jesús T. Piñero, and in 1947 the U.S. Congress allowed Puerto Rico to elect its governors by popular vote. Muñoz Marín was elected in November of the following year, and he took office in January 1949.

For more than a generation the PPD governed Puerto Rico, led mainly by Muñoz Marín during four terms as governor.

During the period 1948–68 Puerto Rico experienced a major economic change, shifting from agricultural dominance to an economy based on industrial production, largely through Operation Bootstrap, a government program that promoted economic development and social welfare.

The program initially promoted cooperative farming and labor-intensive industries, but when these efforts failed, the government invested heavily in transportation infrastructure and attracted privately owned factories through tax breaks and government-supported start-up costs.

These factors, together with low wages on the island, induced hundreds of U.S. (and some European) companies to open factories there. Workers increasingly left the sugarcane and coffee fields and moved into the coastal cities where wages, working conditions, and social services were improved. However, many also migrated to large metropolitan centers in the United States.

Chapter 21

The Commonwealth of Puerto Rico

In addition to reforming the Puerto Rican economy, the PPD modified the island's political relationship with the United States. In October 1950 President Truman signed the Puerto Rico Commonwealth Bill, which enabled the island's people to establish their own constitution. Some Puerto Ricans, notably the Nationalists, opposed the new law and resorted to violence.

A handful of Nationalists unsuccessfully attempted to assassinate Gov. Muñoz Marín in San Juan, and Nationalist uprisings erupted in several island towns, causing 27 deaths. In November two New York-based Nationalists tried to kill Truman in Washington, D.C.

In 1951 Puerto Ricans overwhelmingly approved the commonwealth status in a referendum, and the island's constitution was proclaimed on July 25, 1952, a symbolic date because it was the 54th anniversary of the U.S. invasion of the island. The constitution reaffirmed the post of an elected governor, created a legislative branch in which minority representation was guaranteed, and set up a new judicial system based on civil liberties.

Dissatisfaction continued to be expressed despite broad popular support for the autonomy of the commonwealth government and a rapidly modernizing industrial society. Nationalist violence broke out again on March 1, 1954, in Washington, when four Nationalists, three men and a woman, fired weapons from the viewing galleries of the House of Representatives, wounding five Congressmen.

Legal reviews in the courts, both insular and federal, continued to enforce the commonwealth concept. At the same time, Puerto Ricans were unable to expand the limits of their autonomy to include international diplomacy, such as playing a greater role in Caribbean affairs. Sentiment in favor of statehood grew following the admission of Alaska and Hawaii to the United States, particularly because Puerto Ricans increasingly were depending on federal aid for the unemployed, elderly, and war veterans.

In addition, in 1959 Puerto Ricans became highly concerned over regional security and ideology following Fidel Castro's communist revolution in Cuba, and the island absorbed a sizable influx of Cuban exiles.

Muñoz Marín stepped down in 1964 and was succeeded by his able administrative assistant Roberto Sánchez Vilella, who in November of that year became the second elected governor in the island's history.

However, with the charismatic Muñoz Marín retired from the political scene, the PPD lost its firm grip on power and was fiercely opposed by pro-statehood groups. In 1968 the PPD lost control of the lower house of the legislature after a split in its ranks, and it also relinquished the governorship to Luis A. Ferré, who led the pro-statehood New Progressive Party, Partido Nuevo Progresista; PNP.

Since then, the PPD and PNP have alternated in power....

Puerto Rican society underwent sweeping changes during the 1960s and '70s. Agriculture lost importance, and there was rapid growth in manufacturing and in the number and size of urban and suburban settlements.

In addition, cultural, political, and economic links with the United States increased as greater numbers of Puerto Ricans migrated there.

The U.S. government introduced food stamps in 1974 to improve the diets of poorer residents, and by 1980 about three-fifths of the population was receiving the benefit.

Rafael Hernández Colón

The PPD returned to power briefly in 1973–76 under the leadership of Rafael Hernández Colón, a young protégé of Muñoz Marín. The pro-statehood PNP regained power in 1976 under the vigorous leadership of Carlos Romero Barceló, but Hernández Colón won back the governorship for the PPD in 1984 and served for two terms.

In November 1992 Pedro Rossello, a medical doctor, led the pro-statehood PNP to another electoral victory, and he was reelected governor in 1996. However, a series of corruption scandals soon caused the PNP to lose support.

In November 2000 the mayor of San Juan, Sila Calderón of the pro-commonwealth PPD, was elected as Puerto Rico's first woman governor. The appointment of Sonia Sotomayor, a judge of Puerto Rican descent, to the U.S. Supreme Court in 2009 inspired pride that transcended political affiliation.

The Debate over Political Status

In 1952, after Puerto Rico was granted commonwealth status, the United States advised the United Nations, UN, that the island was a self-governing territory. However, dissatisfaction with the island's political status continued.

A commission appointed by the U.S. Congress concluded that three options—commonwealth, statehood, or independence—should be considered in a plebiscite, which was held in July 1967.

The majority PPD supported the plebiscite, but it was boycotted by the pro-statehood and independence parties. The result showed that 60.4 percent of the electorate supported commonwealth status, 38.9 percent statehood, and 0.6 percent independence. Both the leaders of the PPD and influential members of the U.S. federal government agreed that the commonwealth relationship needed to be improved and the degree of self-government broadened.

However, no other action was taken, partly because political power on the island began to alternate between pro-commonwealth and pro-statehood parties.

After the pro-statehood PNP swept to victory in the 1992 gubernatorial elections, it pushed for a second plebiscite, which was held in November 1993 with nearly three-fourths of the 2.2 million eligible voters taking part; the pro-commonwealth option won by a plurality of 48.6 percent, followed by 46.3 percent for statehood and 4 percent for independence.

When the PNP governor won a second term in 1996, the party mounted a campaign to hold still another plebiscite; however, the PPD, protesting that the definition of commonwealth on the ballot was inadequate, urged its followers to vote for "none of the above.

"In the December 1998 plebiscite, the "none of the above" option won most 50.3 percent of the vote, followed by 46.6 percent for statehood and 2.5 percent for independence, marking the third time in three decades that statehood had been rebuffed by Puerto Rican voters.

In July 1999, Gov. Pedro Rosselló urged the UN decolonization committee to intervene by putting Puerto Rico back on the list of non-self-governing territories.

Until that time, only pro-independence groups had actively lobbied at the UN, decrying Puerto Rico's "colonial" status. Now, pro-statehood activists were joining the effort, out of frustration with Washington's apparent reluctance to either embrace statehood or expand Puerto Rico's autonomous powers.

Washington policymakers, in turn, have highlighted the Puerto Ricans' inability to reach a consensus on political status. Several members of Congress have expressed doubts about the ability of the United States to absorb a Spanish-speaking state, while others have voiced concern that statehood would sharply increase the already large amount of federal funds flowing to the island.

The controversial issue of Vieques, an island municipality of Puerto Rico, has united Puerto Ricans across party lines. The U.S. Navy, which owns two-thirds of Vieques, began military maneuvers there, including bombing practice, in the mid-20th century.

Opposition to the navy's use of the island intensified after two off-target bombs killed a civilian guard on the bombing range in 1999. Protesters subsequently prevented the navy from carrying out many of its maneuvers on Vieques, and Puerto Rican officials of all three major parties cited health and environmental concerns as they lobbied for an end to military exercises there. In 2001 the U.S. government announced plans for a gradual cessation of the maneuvers.

Few Puerto Ricans consider political status to be one of the key problems facing the commonwealth, but the island's leaders continue to push for a resolution. Most of the people clearly value some form of permanent association with the United States, although Puerto Ricans fiercely embrace their language and Hispanic American culture; some have even pointed out that, under statehood, Puerto Rico could no longer field its own teams for the Olympic Games.

As the debate continued into the 21st century, striking parallels could be drawn to the period of Spanish colonial rule, when the choices of full assimilation, statehood, autonomy, commonwealth, or independence for the island were also deliberated.

In November 2012, Puerto Ricans went to the polls for the fourth time in 45 years to attempt to settle the question of the commonwealth's political status. The two-part nonbinding referendum asked voters if they felt Puerto Rico should continue under its present form of territorial status. Some 54 percent of those who voted indicated that they were not satisfied with that status. The second part of the referendum asked voters if they wanted the island to become (1) a U.S. state, (2) an independent country, or (3) a "sovereign free-associated state."

About 61 percent of those who voted chose statehood; however, hundreds of thousands of voters left the question blank, presumably because they had not been offered other non-statehood options, including the possibility of remaining a commonwealth. In the eyes of many U.S. lawmakers, those limited choices brought into question whether a majority of Puerto Ricans wanted statehood.

The island's political status was a pivotal element in the financial crisis that reached a crescendo at the end of June 2015, when Gov. Alejandro García Padilla announced that Puerto Rico could no longer meet its debt obligations. Although not a U.S. state, Puerto Rico was treated like a state and not a municipality under the U.S. federal bankruptcy code and therefore could not declare bankruptcy.

Repeated attempts to balance Puerto Rico's budget through austerity measures, tax increases, and further borrowing had failed to arrest its debt spiral, and García Padilla called on creditors to restructure his government's debt and beseeched the federal government to make it possible for the commonwealth to declare bankruptcy.

Because Puerto Rican bonds were widely held and, were common elements of many mutual funds, the potential ripple impact of the crisis on the U.S. economy was significant.

At the end of June 2016, U.S. Pres. Barack Obama signed into law the Puerto Rico Oversight, Management and Economic Stability Act (PROMESA), which authorized the Puerto Rican government to restructure more than $70 billion in debt.

The act also created a federally appointed seven-member oversight board to control Puerto Rico's finances, a stipulation that was only grudgingly accepted by García Padilla, who chose not to run for reelection. In November

Ricardo Rosselló, a pro-statehood candidate, was elected to succeed García Padilla.

Violence in Puerto Rico is horrible; however, nature's
rage is worst. I had to mention the hurricanes....
These two beauties nearly destroyed the whole island...

Hurricanes Maria and Fiona
Puerto Rico: Hurricane Maria

On September 20, 2017, Puerto Rico was hammered by Hurricane Maria, a near category 5 cyclone that produced winds of up to 155 miles (250 km) per hour and dropped some 30 inches, 750 mm of rain on parts of the island in just one day.

The devastation produced by the storm was massive; the damage was estimated at more than $90 billion. Much of Puerto Rico's outdated electricity infrastructure was destroyed; as late as nearly five months after the storm, some 400,000 of the island's electricity customers still were without power. The official count of deaths that resulted from the disaster was 64, but some estimates attributed more than 1,000 deaths to the storm.

In August 2018 the commonwealth government raised the official death toll to nearly 3,000. That figure was based on the results of a study that the government had commissioned from the Milken Institute School of Public Health at the George Washington University, which concluded that the initial official count had considered only those who were killed directly by the hurricane, through drowning or injury by collapsed buildings or flying wreckage, and failed to consider the fatalities resulting from the long-term, six-month, consequences of the disaster.

On September 18, 2022, Puerto Rico was again hit by a hurricane. Although not as strong as Maria, Hurricane Fiona caused flooding and landslides, and it knocked out the island's electricity.

Chapter 22

Ponce, Puerto Rico

Puerto Rican Police Officer Held in Fatal Shooting of 3 Colleagues
A police officer who once had his department-issued firearm taken away while he underwent psychological treatment gunned down two superiors and a third colleague at a regional headquarters in this southern Puerto Rico city, police officials said.

By the way, I saw all the running around from my window. This police headquarters is right here, in Los Caobos...

The shooting was another setback for a police agency so rife with corruption and reports of excessive force that the federal Department of Justice in 2011 called it "broken in critical and fundamental respects."

The officer, Guarionex Candelario Rivera, 50, a 19-year veteran of the Puerto Rico Police, an agency comparable to the state police elsewhere, showed up at the Ponce headquarters about 9:30 a.m. and asked for an appointment with personnel supervisors, a police spokesman, Sgt. Axel Valencia, said.

Shortly afterward, armed with a gun and a knife, Officer Candelario shot and killed a commander, Frank Román; a personnel lieutenant, Luz M. Soto, 49, a 23-year veteran of the department who recently passed an exam to become a captain; and Rosario Hernández, 42, a uniformed officer who had worked there for 15 years, the police said.

The two higher-ranking victims worked in the administrative division and did not supervise the suspect, the police said.

Department officials confirmed that Officer Candelario was under guard Monday night while hospitalized for multiple gunshot wounds sustained during the encounter.

Officer Candelario had been on medical leave for about a year and a half because of psychological problems and had been forced to surrender his weapon, Sergeant Valencia confirmed.

His department-issued firearm was later returned to him after police psychologists determined that he was fit for duty.

"The same psychologists recommended to the police that he was ready to be armed again," Sergeant Valencia said. "The Police Department does not rearm any police officer until they have gone through the proper protocol: a medical exam or psychological exam. Obviously, the police personnel are stunned by what happened, shocked, saddened."

Hector Agosto, the colonel in charge of the station, stood before reporters with blood on his shirt and declined to provide more information.

The details of the shooting were still undetermined because the police station had been evacuated at the time because of a suspicious package, a police spokeswoman said.

Investigators were prevented from examining the crime scene for an hour and a half, the authorities said. A motive is still being sought, Sergeant Valencia said.

"He already had emotional problems and high stress levels," said Ismael Rivera, the president of the Union of Puerto Rican Police in Ponce. "Then, without justification of any kind, he acted in the way he did, taking the lives of three people."

Mr. Rivera said the suspect had recently been informed of some kind of investigation against him. He said that in 2010, a police psychologist issued a report showing that 82 percent of Puerto Rico's police officers suffered from "emotional burnout syndrome." More than 40 percent of the officers had acute symptoms, Mr. Rivera said.

The Puerto Rico Police Department is known for low pay and high levels of corruption. In September, the F.B.I. arrested 10 police officers, accusing them of stealing drugs and money. In 2013, the agency entered a consent decree with the Justice Department, which found systemic use of force and violations of the Constitution. Cesar Miranda,

Puerto Rico's justice secretary said the Civil Rights Division of the Justice Department had been notified and would also investigate all the killings. The governor of Puerto Rico, Alejandro García Padilla, told reporters gathered outside the police station that "the Police Department will continue giving the maximum, will continue the street fighting crime and will continue doing everything it was doing to reform itself and give good results to the country.

Juanita Alfonso, a police officer who knew the suspect and the victims, described her fallen colleagues as family who shared "blue blood." The staff had been preparing a holiday lunch when the killings occurred, she said.

"These hurts too much," Officer Alfonso said. "We just want you to know that our police officers in this precinct are people of excellence. This happened, just as it can happen in any family. We want people to understand that we are also going through many problems, and we have such a difficult job."

Chapter 23

Puerto Rico Line of Duty Deaths

NOEL DAVID CORDERO-GUZMÁN

Sergeant Noel Cordero-Guzmán was shot and killed with his own weapon after intervening in a disturbance while off duty.

He was at a local fast-food restaurant with friends when he observed a group of people creating a disturbance. Sergeant Cordero-Guzmán had a previous encounter with one of the men causing the disturbance.

After identifying himself with the group, he was attacked and beaten. One of the suspects then grabbed Sergeant Cordero-Guzmán's service weapon and shot him in the chest, killing him.

The 17-year-old shooter was charged as an adult with first-degree murder, attempted murder, and weapons violations. He was sentenced to 109 years in prison.

Sergeant Cordero-Guzmán had served with the Ponce Municipal Police Department for two years. He is survived by his expectant wife and 5-year-old child.

He was posthumously promoted to the rank of sergeant.

ALVIN R. SUGRAÑES-LEBRÓN

Sergeant Alvin Sugrañes-Lebrón was shot and killed at the main gate of the Guayama 500 Correctional Institution by a disgruntled corrections officer who worked at another facility.

Undiscovered to Sergeant Sugrañes-Lebrón the officer had just murdered another member of the agency whom he was romantically involved with and a neighbor. The officer was denied access to the facility after demanding to see other officers assigned there.

Sergeant Sugrañes-Lebrón told the officer to wait as he requested another supervisor to respond to the post to speak to him.

As the other supervisor approached the officer opened fire, killing Sergeant Sugrañes-Lebrón. The man fled into a nearby wooded area where he remained in hiding for two days. He committed suicide while members of a fugitive task force negotiated with him.

Sergeant Sugrañes-Lebrón is survived by his wife and child.

IRVING GONZALEZ

Correctional Officer Irving Gonzalez was shot to death after being attacked by a prisoner during a transport from the Rio Piedras State Prison to the Bayamon District Courthouse for the prisoner's murder trial.

The transport vehicle was being driven by a prison trustee and Officer Gonzalez was riding in the front passenger seat. The prisoner, who was handcuffed in the front and sitting behind Officer Gonzalez, pulled a shank out of his afro-style hair and stabbed Officer Gonzalez in the eye. He was then able to disarm Officer Gonzalez and he ordered the trustee out of the vehicle before driving it away.

Officer Gonzalez's body was in the vehicle a short distance away suffering from a gunshot wound to the abdomen.

The prisoner was arrested several days later and returned to prison. On January 5th, 1979, he and two other inmates at the Bayamon

Correctional Complex murdered Correctional Officer Anibal Ramos-Feliciano and Correctional Officer Angel Morales during an escape attempt.

The other two inmates were eventually recaptured but Officer Gonzalez's murderer remains at large.

Officer Gonzalez had served with the Puerto Rico Department of Corrections and Rehabilitation for 11 years.

VICTOR M. ANDORNO-TORRES

Deputy Marshal Andorno-Torres and Deputy Marshal Pascual Gomez-Lopez were shot and killed when they interrupted a robbery in progress at a local restaurant.

The marshals were serving summonses and had stopped at the restaurant to ask for directions to the location indicated on the summonses. The suspects disarmed both marshals and then fatally shot them.

The suspects were apprehended and convicted of two counts of first-degree murder. They were sentenced to life in prison without parole.

Deputy Marshal Andorno-Torres had served with the agency for 7 years.

PASCUAL GOMEZ-LOPEZ

Deputy Marshal Gomez-Lopez and Deputy Marshal Victor Andorno-Torres were shot and killed when they interrupted a robbery in progress at a local restaurant. The two officers were serving summonses and had stopped at the restaurant to ask for directions to a particular location.

The marshals were serving summonses and had stopped at the restaurant to ask for directions to the location indicated on the summonses. The suspects disarmed both marshals and then fatally shot them.

The suspects were apprehended and convicted of two counts of first-degree murder. They were sentenced to life in prison without parole.

Deputy Marshal Gomez-Lopez had served with the Puerto Rico Commonwealth Marshal's Office for 8 years.

ANIBAL RAMOS-FELICIANO

Correctional Officer Anibal Ramos-Feliciano and Correctional Officer Angel "Moralito" Morales were shot and killed inside the Bayamon Correctional Complex by an inmate who was attempting to escape with two other inmates.

The inmate had previously been convicted of two murders, including the murder of Correctional Officer Irving Gonzalez during a previous escape on May 3rd, 1975. As Officer Morales and Officer Ramos-Feliciano entered the gallery area of Annex 308 for a routine inspection they were attacked by the three inmates.

The inmate who had previously murdered Officer Gonzalez had obtained a revolver that had been smuggled into the prison and shot both officers in the head, killing them.

All three inmates were able to escape after climbing over the wall of the prison and shooting at the guards in the watchtower. Two of the inmates were arrested several days later but the inmate who had murdered Officer Gonzalez, Officer Morales, and Officer Ramos-Feliciano was never apprehended and remains at large.

Officer Ramos-Feliciano had served with the Puerto Rico Department of Corrections and Rehabilitation for only six months and had previously served with the Puerto Rico Police Department.

In 2010 the Puerto Rico Department of Corrections and Rehabilitation renamed their training academy the Ramos and Morales Correctional Officers Academy.

Chapter 24

In Alaska

CURTIS MATTHEW WORLAND

Court Services Officer Curtis Worland died from injuries he received when a musk ox attacked him near Nome.

Officer Worland was using his snowmobile to scare the musk oxen away from his dog mushing team while on a paid work break.

A musk ox charged him, and the horn punctured his leg, striking his femoral artery. Officer Worland drove away from the musk ox but was found unresponsive near his snowmobile at 1:30 pm.

Officer Worland had served with the Alaska State Troopers for 13 years. He is survived by his wife, parents, and siblings.

In Pennsylvania

Chief of Police Justin McIntire
Brackenridge Borough Police Department, Pennsylvania

End of Watch Monday, January 2, 2023

JUSTIN MCINTIRE

Chief of Police Justin McIntire was shot and killed near the intersection of Brackenridge Avenue and Morgan Street during a foot pursuit of a wanted subject.

The man was wanted for a probation violation involving weapons and had fled from the Pennsylvania State Police during a traffic stop the previous night. He then fled on foot from Harrison Township the following morning during a traffic stop. At about 2:00 pm he was located near the border of Brackenridge Borough and Tarentum Borough and led officers on a foot pursuit for over two hours.

He opened fire on officers in the 900 block of Brackenridge Avenue and again in the 800 block of 3rd Avenue in which Chief McIntire was killed and a Tarentum Borough officer was wounded.

After shooting both officers the man carjacked a vehicle and fled into the city of Pittsburgh. He fled into a wooded area following a vehicle pursuit and then opened fire on officers. He was shot and killed by return fire.

Chief McIntire had been sworn in as police chief of the Brackenridge Borough Police Department exactly four years earlier.

Deputy Sheriff Isaiah Cordero
Riverside County Sheriff's Department, California

End of Watch Thursday, December 29, 2022

ISAIAH CORDERO

Deputy Sheriff Isaiah Cordero was shot and killed while making a traffic stop in the 3900 block of Golden West Avenue in the Jurupa Valley area.

Deputy Cordero was approaching the vehicle he had stopped when the driver pulled out a gun and opened fire on him, fatally wounding him. A citizen who witnessed the shooting called 911 and rendered aide until other deputies arrived.

The subject fled the scene and then led officers on a vehicle pursuit that spanned multiple counties. The subject's vehicle became disabled, and he was then shot and killed after he opened fire on officers. The man had an extensive criminal history and had stabbed a California Highway Patrol canine in 2021.

At the time of Deputy Cordero's murder, the man was out on bail even after having been arrested for failing to appear while awaiting a mandatory 25-years to life sentence for the incident in which he stabbed the canine.

Deputy Cordero had served with the Riverside County Sheriff's Department for 8-1/2 years and was assigned to the Motor Unit. He is survived by his parents and stepbrother.

Chapter 25

Canada

Police Officers killed while on duty

The shooting death of Ontario Provincial Police Const. Grzegorz Pierzchala mere hours after he had passed his 10-month probation period and was granted the ability to patrol independently, has left many in the ranks devastated.

OPP say Pierzchala, 28, was shot just after 2:30 p.m. ET on Tuesday while responding to a vehicle in a ditch just west of Hagersville, about 45 kilometres southwest of Hamilton.

He is the fourth officer to be killed while on duty in Ontario this fall and the fifth killed in Canada while on the job since mid-September. Another officer was killed in a car collision while off duty, allegedly by an impaired driver.

"This is unprecedented in Canada," said Mark Baxter, president of the Police Association of Ontario, which represents 28,000 sworn members from 45 police associations across the province.

Man and woman charged with 1st-degree murder in shooting of OPP officer near Brantford Slain Haldimand OPP officer was living 'his dream' to work with police "I've been in policing for 18 years, but certainly during my time I've never seen anything like this," said Baxter.

"It really has shaken our profession to the core."

In Ontario between 1961 and 2009, data from Statistics Canada show 44 homicides against police officers, a rate of less than one per year.

Between 2010 and 2021, five officers were killed in Ontario, including Const. Marc Hovingh and Const. Jeffrey Northrup in 2020 and 2021, respectively.

"We hear about the deaths of police officers in the United States just south of us far too frequently. This doesn't happen in Canada," Baxter said.

"To have all of these deaths in such a short period of time is really quite alarming."

Timeline of 2022 police killings in Canada:

Const. Andrew Hong, 48, of the Toronto Police Service was fatally shot in a Mississauga, Ont., coffee shop on Sept. 12.

Const. Morgan Russell, 54, and Const. Devon Northrup, 33, of the South Simcoe Police Service both died in hospital after responding to a call at a home in Innisfail, Ont., located about 100 kilometers north of Toronto, on Oct. 11.

Const. Shaelyn Yang, 31, was working on a mental health and outreach team when she was stabbed to death on Oct. 18 in Burnaby, B.C.

Const. Grzegorz Pierzchala, 28, was shot and killed while responding to a vehicle in a ditch just west of Hagersville, Ont., on Dec. 27.

The list does not include Const. Travis Gillespie, 38, a York Regional Police officer who was allegedly killed by an impaired driver in a head-on collision on his way to work in Markham on Sept. 14.

StatsCan says the police officers killed were on average 34 years old at the time of their death and had been with their present police service for a period of less than five years.

Michael Arntfield, a criminologist and professor at Western University, says the recent deaths are concerning and an indication of how dangerous policing has become, given the growing responsibilities of officers.

But Arntfield, a former officer himself, says police deaths are still rare and the string of tragedies does not represent a growing trend. Supports available, police associations said.

However, as police services across provinces grapple with the number of officers killed this year, Ontario Provincial Police Association spokesperson Scott Mills says police agencies rally around each other for support.

"It doesn't matter what service you work for. It just strikes you right in the heart, like it's one of your own family members that died," says Mills.

OPP officer killed near Brantford, Ont., while responding to a call, commissioner says.

He says the 'Encompas' Mental Health Wellness Program is available to 6,200 uniform and approximately 3,600 civilian members of the OPPA.

Some of the other services available, Mills says, include:

#HealthyWorkplaceTeam, which serves Ontario Provincial Police members, families, retirees, and auxiliaries

OPP Beyond the Blue, which focuses on the wellbeing of OPP officers and their families.

Canada Beyond the Blue, which provides community support to police spouses and families.

Boots on the Ground, an anonymous peer support for first responders.

Badge of Life Canada, which helps Canadian public safety personnel and their families who are dealing with operational stress injuries, including post-traumatic stress.

Pierzchala's death comes as police agencies are grappling with staffing shortages and recruitment issues across the country, an issue Mills says may be affected by the latest killings.

"There are so many lines of duty deaths and it is taking a toll. Our staffing levels are low," Mills said.

Baxter says every police department in the province is understaffed and experiencing a staffing crisis.

"And on top of that, we are having recruiting challenges already and we know that these types of events only compound that," says Baxter.

Five Canadian Police Officers Killed

Four on-duty Canadian police officers and one off-duty officer have been killed in just 37 days, leaving families and communities reeling with grief across the country.

Const. Shaelyn Yang was stabbed to death in Burnaby on Tuesday after responding to a park where a person experiencing homelessness was living.

Yang, 31, was a resident of Richmond and had been an RCMP member for just shy of three years.

"She was a loving wife, a sister, and a daughter," says Deputy Commissioner Dwayne McDonald, BC RCMP Commanding Officer.

"Const. Yang was a kind and compassionate person, which makes her death even more difficult to accept. Her loss is immeasurable."

Robert Gordon, a criminology professor at Simon Fraser University, says officers being killed on duty is rare and not something we should expect to see continue.

"This is unusual, fortunately; we don't see this kind of activity, these tragedies that often," says Gordon. "I don't see that this is a national trend of any kind."

He added the killings will ultimately impact how police officers conduct themselves and do their job.

"Police officers now have to be doubly careful about how they proceed into potentially volatile situations," he says. "Especially where there's any suggestion that, or possibility, that the person is impaired in some way either because of a mental illness or an ingestion of drugs or excessive amounts of alcohol."

The recent killings of officers also highlight the "inaction" of dealing with homelessness, according to Gordon.

"They're people in extreme need, and we're not addressing those needs properly and we've allowed 'we' are being the community — these sub-communities to develop and to become established," he says. "The minute you don't move on those situations and allow them to grow, with the best of intentions, you are building a problem."

Former B.C. solicitor general and West Vancouver police chief Kash Heed says every officer should be able to return home to their loved ones after their shift, without being harmed.

"Most telling, is the mental health issue and the fact that we've been talking so much about this, but very little action on dealing with it," Heed told Glacier Media.

"We've got people with severe emotional health issues that are not being dealt with in a comprehensive nature. And as a result, they're out there in society roaming our streets, and look at the unfortunate incident that happened to those young police officer yesterday in Burnaby."

The newly elected Richmond city councilor says the current system is at a tipping point, but questions if it will be enough to create real change.

"The death of a police officer so tragically, which, in my humble opinion, most likely could have been prevented, should be a wake-up call. Do I think it's going to resonate in their minds? No," he says.

Heed is calling for more support for people struggling with mental health.

"Immediately, what we need to do is make sure that we have a facility that we can take these people to on a temporary basis. If we must open up a temporary facility while we are building a more modern contemporary facility to treat people with mental health problems, let's do that," says Heed.

Building more spaces to house the homeless or simply hiring more staff won't address the deeper issue, he adds.

"We can hire 200 or 300 more police officers, 200 or 300 more health workers.

It will not make a difference unless we put those other supports in place."

Police officers across Canada mourned the death of Toronto Police Const. Andrew Hong, who was fatally shot while at a Mississauga Tim Hortons on Sept. 12.

"While on lunch break, he was shot in an unprovoked, and may I say, an ambush attack," said Chief Nishan Duraiappah during a press conference.

Days later, on Sept. 14, York Regional Police Const. Travis Gillespie died in Markham, Ont. while driving to work. He was off duty.

On Oct. 11, two officers responded to a disturbance at a house in Innisfail, Ont. Const. Devon Northrup and Const. Morgan Russell from South Simcoe Police Service were both shot, and neither drew their gun. Both police officers died in the hospital.

Back in B.C., condolences are pouring in for Yang and flowers are being placed at the crime scene.

At the time, Yang was working on the mental health and homeless outreach team when she was killed.

"Working with mental health and homelessness can be challenging, but Shaelyn embraced that job with passion. She found value working with this team and working with those struggling in our community," says Chief Supt. Graham de la Gorgendiere, Burnaby RCMP Detachment Commander.

Heed is calling on the B.C. government to make changes.

"We need these politicians to stand up and deal with this," says Heed. "The tragic loss of another police officer, one is far too many. But this is a real tragedy. And if this isn't the tipping point, I'm not sure what's going to be."

The Independent Investigations Office is currently looking into Yang's death. On Wednesday, a 37-old-man was charged with first-degree murder in connection to her death.

Chapter 26

People Murdered in New York City

If you're talking about New York State, the average is closer to 1.5 per day, suggesting that about half of the homicides in the state take place in New York City which is reasonable, since roughly half the population of the state lives there.

Now, to be fair, those numbers consider only the boundaries of New York City itself. The greater New York metro area is somewhat harder to define, because it consists of different municipalities spread across different states.

NYC itself has about 8.5 million people, depending on your definition, the entire metro area contains up to 20 million, extending into New Jersey, Connecticut, even Pennsylvania.

That expanded area would naturally include more homicides, just because it contains more people (more than most countries, in fact). It's possible that this expanded area has a higher homicide rate than NYC proper, but it's probably more or less in the same ballpark.

Now, if a homicide a day seems high to you, you're probably either not from the US, or not understanding the scope of the city. On the other hand, if it seems too low which the putting of the question would imply, it's quite possible that you have an outdated view of the city.

Many people seem to have a view of American crime that was formed in the 70's and 80's and hasn't changed with the times.

For some reason that isn't entirely clear because there are too many theories, not too few, the crime rate across the country rose, rather precipitously, starting in the 1960's, stayed rather shockingly high throughout the 70's and 80's, and then started to quickly decline in the 90's. American homicide rates are still high compared to other wealthy countries, but it's far better than it was.

New York City seems to have gotten particularly bad during that era. A highly concentrated population can be subjected to particularly bad social conditions. The nation's economic woes of the 70's seem to have hit the city particularly badly, with some areas absolutely devastated.

First heroin and then crack became epidemic, and crime became everywhere. During that era, one would certainly expect multiple killings on an average day.

But times have changed. The nation's homicide rate is about a quarter of what it was in the 1990's. New York City has, by all accounts, been cleaned up in every sense. While there are certainly still poor areas, and there are certainly still areas with crime problems, the city is now generally safe. A day with multiple killings would be less common than a day with none.

NYPD Announces Citywide Crime Statistics for July 2022 August 5, 2022

For the month of July 2022, the number of overall shooting incidents increased in New York City compared with July 2021, highlighting the continuing need to eliminate gun violence and end the perception among criminals that there are no consequences for violent crimes.

Citywide shooting incidents increased by 13.4%, 178 v. 157, driven by upticks in Brooklyn, southern Queens, and Staten Island.

Additionally, the number of murders citywide increased for the month by 34.3%, 47 v. 35, compared to the same period last year.

In its continuing effort to stop New Yorkers from being victimized by violence, the NYPD has seized more than 4,300 firearms year-to-date in 2022.

At the same time, citywide gun arrests through July are at a 27-year high, rising to 2,752, which is a 2.4% increase compared with the 2,687-gun arrests through the first seven months of 2021.

Additionally, NYPD officers in July 2022 made 4,017 arrests for complaints of major felony crimes, an 18.2% increase over the 3,398 arrests for major felonies in the same month last year. Arrests for major felonies are up nearly 29% so far in calendar 2022, compared with the first seven months of 2021.

Overall index crime in New York City increased in July 2022, by 30.5% compared with July 2021, 11,619 v. 8,906. Six of the seven major index-crime categories saw increases, driven by a 40.6% increase in grand larceny, 4,588 v.

3,262, a 37.2% increase in robbery, 1,730 v. 1,261, and a 25.6% rise in burglary, 1,325 v. 1,055.

"We know that any crime increase in our city is entirely unacceptable," said Police Commissioner Keechant L. Sewell. "Everyone who lives, works, and visits here deserves to be safe, and the members of the NYPD will tolerate nothing less, but we cannot do it alone.

When violent criminals are willing to carry illegal guns on their streets and brazenly shoot at innocent people, they must face real consequences. When extensive, revolving-door repetition wears away the public's trust in the criminal justice system.

They must make efforts to refocus that system on what matters most: the victims. All residents need to be pulling in the same direction, so that they can best deliver on the public-safety promise we make to every New Yorker, every day."

The precision-policing based enforcement that was carried out in July 2022 continues the NYPD's mission to keep people safe and hold criminals accountable for their crimes.

That work has driven an 8.7% reduction in shootings year-to-date – with 63 fewer shooting victims through the first seven months of 2022 compared to the same period last year and a 4.2% decrease in murders year-to-date through the end of July.

This summer, the NYPD is continuing its work to develop and investigate intelligence-based, long-term cases focused on the few New Yorkers willing to pick up a gun and use it. Much of this work is carried out in concert with the department's law enforcement partners, illustrated by the recent takedown of a violent Trinitarios street crew by our NYPD investigators working alongside the U.S. Attorney's office, the Manhattan District Attorney's office, and the Drug Enforcement Administration.

The NYPD's Gun Violence Suppression Section continues to build strong cases by locating and seizing illegal firearms and in many instances removing them before they can ever be sold on New York City's streets.

The department is committed to our flexible, adaptable approach to shifting crime trends and conditions, and this is evident in the continued implementation of the Summer Violence Reduction Plan.

They are deploying additional officers every day in the precincts, transit districts, and housing developments that need them most. Our summer beach detail, which runs through Labor Day, provides additional coverage for certain commands during the busiest, most crowded time of the year at our city's public beaches.

They have increased patrols in Highways and Traffic Safety officers, Neighborhood Coordination Officers, Field Intelligence Officers, and more. All of this has one goal: keeping every New Yorker safe, in every New York City neighborhood.

This work is ongoing, and always driven by community concerns. The support and partnership the NYPD receives from the community were highlighted citywide on August 2 during the annual "National Night Out Against Crime" events, several of which were attended by the Mayor and Police Commissioner.

Furthermore, they announced the expansion of their highly successful "Saturday Night Lights" program in early July increasing their available gyms by 30% across the city.

This program offers exceptional athletic programs and activities, as well as high-quality coaches and mentors, to children in all five boroughs. They are highly invested in providing the youth with fun, safe, engaging summer pursuits and by centering on youth development, they will continue to build trust and create opportunities for young people in many of the communities that need them most.

The NYPD will never stop fighting for New Yorkers and will always work to keep the criminal justice system's focus where it belongs: on the people they serve.

Chapter 27

Shooting in New York City

Man, 22, Fatally Shot Near Times Square During Rush Hour

The police were searching for two gunmen after the shooting on Eighth Avenue near 44th Street. The victim was not immediately identified.

A 22-year-old man was shot and killed near a Shake Shack in Midtown Manhattan during the evening rush hour on Thursday, and police were searching for two gunmen hours later.

The shooting occurred at about 5:30 p.m. around West 44th Street and Eighth Avenue in the Times Square area, the police said. Officers responding to a 911 call found the man with a gunshot wound to the chest, and he was taken to Mount Sinai West, where he died.

The police had blocked off the sidewalk in front of the theater district outpost of the Shake Shack fast-food chain, and the normally bustling shop was closed on Thursday night. At least one shell casing was visible on 44th Street, and foot traffic was being redirected along Eighth Avenue.

A bouncer at Smith's, a bar across the street, said he heard a single shot and saw people running, and the police arrived shortly after. The victim was not immediately identified, and the police were searching for the "unknown perpetrators" on Thursday night.

The shooting took place in one of the city's busiest sections, just steps from Broadway theaters, hotels, the sprawling Times Square subway station and the Port Authority Bus Terminal.

The area had struggled as the pandemic kept away tourists and office workers, and its recovery has been dogged by concerns about crime amid a citywide uptick. Though shootings and murders dropped last year, major crime was still up 22 percent.

At the same time, about 56 million people visited the city in 2022, according to NYC & Company, the city's tourism agency, a dramatic increase from 2021. The return of visitors brought New York to 85 percent of prepandemic tourism levels, and the agency expects the number to rise further this year.

Two tourists visiting from Scotland, Isla Cleland and Marcus Lavery, were shocked to learn of the shooting as they walked through the area on their way to dinner on their first night in Manhattan.

"Oh my god," Ms. Cleland thought to herself. "That's just not normal."

"Mental," said Mr. Lavery. "Good place, though."

Kees Van Liempt, 69, said he was visiting from the Netherlands to spend time with his wife and daughter. His four days spent in the city, he said, were "too long."

Mr. Van Liempt initially planned to eat at the Shake Shack before going to see a play with them. He noticed the police presence as soon as he exited the subway around 6 p.m.

"Another day in New York," he said. "That's what you hear all day when you live in New York. Sirens, or police, or ambulance, or firemen, or whatever. That's what you hear in New York."

More Shooting in the Street of NYC

One hundred and forty nine Shot, sixteen Dead: Gunfire's Rising Toll on New York City's Youngest.

Shayma Roman was among nearly 150 shooting victims under the age of 18 this year. Her family and friends are trying to chart a path forward.

The laughter of sisters once filled the bedroom as they jumped and danced to 1990s R&B. Shayma and Tayma Roman were known around the neighborhood as twins even though they were about two years apart: One was rarely spotted without the other close by.

Their room sat silent in early October.

Shayma, a 17-year-old cheerleader, basketball player and fashion lover, had been in front of her grandmother's apartment in Crown Heights, Brooklyn, with her sister Tayma, 19, when gunmen opened fire on Sept. 28, hitting her in the torso. Shayma, who relatives said was held in Tayma's arms as she bled, died at Brookdale Hospital.

Tayma didn't come to a memorial service days later a misty October night. It was too difficult for her to return home, family said. Instead, she was mourning blocks away, surrounded by friends.

"They shared a room all of their life," said Shakim-Unique Correnthi, their older brother. "They were together 24/7."

There have been 149 shooting victims under 18 this year, as of Dec. 18, according to Police Department data. That's notably higher than the number in 2021, when 138 children were shot.

In 2017, when gun violence hit historic lows, just 75 shooting victims were children.

The number of people under 18 charged in shootings is also rising: 105 were reported through the end of September, compared with 102 in all of 2021, according to the most recent data provided by the Police Department.

"The increase including the youth is incredibly tragic, scary," said Michael-Sean Spence, senior director for community safety initiatives at Everytown for Gun Safety. "The increase has been the highest over the last five years amongst those under the age of 18."

Experts name several reasons: the pandemic's upheaval in school and home lives; the proliferation of guns; and the economic devastation of low-income communities over the past three years.

Community leaders have said that scant resources for academic support, after-school programs and mental health services have left children aimless and caught in cycles of violence and revenge.

In 2020, firearm fatalities became the leading cause of death for young people between ages 1 and 19 in the United States, surpassing motor vehicle crashes.

The rate at which gun deaths rose for children and adolescents between 2019 and 2020 was more than twice as high as the increase among the general population. Black children have been disproportionately affected.

Between 2018 and 2021, firearm deaths doubled among Black youth and rose by 50 percent among Hispanic youth, according to the Kaiser Family Foundation. Boys were four times more likely than girls to die.

In New York's communities most affected by violence, memorials of devotional candles, stuffed animals, balloons, and handwritten notes propped up under smiling pictures of those killed have become commonplace.

The stories begin to echo as the numbers grow.

Days before Shayma was killed, 17-year-old Jordany Aracena was fatally shot in front of his home in the Bronx neighborhood of Mott Haven. A 17-year-old boy was charged with murder.

Prince Shabazz and Jacob Borbin from the Bronx and Justin Streeter from Harlem were also killed this year. They were all 14.

"I've seen so many young people just destroyed," said Oresa Napper-Williams, founder of Not Another Child, a nonprofit based in Brooklyn. Ms. Napper-Williams started the organization in 2006 after her 21-year-old son, Andrell Daron Napper, was killed by a stray bullet from a gunshot by a 15-year-old.

"Their mental capacity with all of this gun violence hearing the guns and still having to get up and go to school the next day and walking over the blood of somebody that may have been killed the night before," she said.

In late November, sitting in the house where Shayma lived, her aunt, Shanikka Harrison, talked about how their lives had changed.

Ms. Harrison, a mother of eight who lives in Long Island, inherited a variety of roles after her niece's killing: spokeswoman, resource navigator and chauffeur. She drove her sister, Shayma's mother, to appointments including those at the funeral home.

Shayma's funeral in October was filled with mourners. But two months later, things are quieter, and the family's concern is growing for the siblings, cousins and friends left behind, Ms. Harrison said.

"They're going to be changed forever," she said.

Shayma's sister returned to the bedroom about two weeks before Thanksgiving, after it was redecorated, and a small memorial was added. However, Tayma has become isolated, her aunt said. Her brother and cousins have become anxious about walking the streets they grew up in.

When she was killed, Shayma was just days from her 18th birthday and months from graduating from high school. She had transferred to Brooklyn Democracy Academy in Brownsville, an alternative for students struggling in traditional schools, and was focused on a newfound dream of college, her family said.

Now, many friends have had to be persuaded into going back to school or resuming work, Ms. Harrison said.

Students who are repeatedly exposed to violent crime in their neighborhoods score lower on standardized tests than their peers, especially in reading, according to a study of New York City students published last year.

The more often that children are exposed to violence, the further they fall behind, researchers found.

Overall crime in the city has dramatically declined since the 1980s and 1990s, and this year, shootings and murders decreased from last year as pandemic-era spikes receded: The number of people shot fell by about 17 percent, while homicides dropped by roughly 13 percent.

New York City and State have announced millions in funding for anti-violence programs. In December of last year alone, the city was awarded a $20.5 million grant from the federal government to invest in violence prevention, specifically for young people.

Mr. Adams expanded a summer jobs program, as well as Saturday Night Lights, which offers activities for children between the ages of 11 and 18. And the Police Department said in a prepared statement that it "routinely collaborates.

With violence interrupters, local clergy, local organizations, community stakeholders and other city agencies to stem youth violence."

This spring, the mayor launched a Gun Violence Prevention Task Force, which he said at the time would "address the root causes of gun violence and prevent shootings before they take place." The task force has met consistently, said

Jonah Allon, a deputy press secretary. He gave no specifics about what results it had produced or whether it would propose specific initiatives or plans.

"Shootings across the city are down by double digits this year and we have removed nearly 7,000 illegal guns from the streets," Mr. Allon said. "We will continue to build on the productive steps we've taken this year and continue to invest in a holistic vision of public safety that keeps our youngest safe from the scourge of gun violence."

Residents do what they can. In Brooklyn, leaders in Shayma's neighborhood organized a vigil. Students at her school released balloons. Another high school in Crown Heights, Explore Empower Charter School, held a walkout to raise awareness about gun violence and pay tribute to its victims, including Shayma.

Children and adults at the events, many of whom had lost loved ones to guns, expressed frustration at the violence. They were not experts or policymakers, but there was a sense of resolve that if enough voices pleaded for solutions, the killings might decrease.

"New members keep being added to these events and it's heartbreaking," Ms. Harrison said.

On a Monday in mid-November, Ms. Harrison appeared at a community council meeting in the 77th Precinct, where Shayma was killed. She had written several drafts of the message she wanted residents, community leaders and police officers to hear.

"My family and I will get through the toughest battle we have yet to face," she had written. "We can do this partially, knowing our community is working diligently to empower our children by providing them new improved programs and resources. Ensuring a safer and more productive future."

But when Ms. Harrison stood to deliver the message, her tongue failed her. She was unable to speak. "I couldn't get it out at all," she said later. "I couldn't even say my name." As she wept at the meeting, an organizer stepped in to read her message for her.

Chapter 28

NYPD Ways to End Gun Violence

New York City has been tested to its core in the first month of 2022. These weeks have been among the most violent in recent memory, most of it caused by a crisis of gun violence that continues to plague our communities. Every New Yorker has been reminded.

Gun violence is an epidemic that does not discriminate. It has tragically reached our NYPD officers, our young people working late to support their families, and even a child not yet one year old.

Gun violence is a public health crisis that continues to threaten every corner of NYC.

It has not emerged out of nowhere. Over the past several years, a small population of individuals has driven a massive increase in violence in our city. There is no single cause for the systemic gun violence that has taken far too many lives, but to move beyond this moment, to end this painful chapter, will take all of us.

This blueprint has been in the works since the earliest days of Mayor Adams' campaign. The Adams Administration has made public safety and justice its highest priorities knowing these are prerequisites to prosperity in New York.

Mayor Adams came into office determined to remove guns from our streets, protect our communities, and create a safe, prosperous city for all New Yorkers.

THE CHALLENGE

The sea of gun violence in NYC does not have one single point of origin. It flows from many rivers, each contributing to the problem. To address a challenge of this magnitude, we must block every river that has fed into this crisis: a pandemic that has severed fragile social bonds; schools and governments that have for too long failed our young people, especially young men of color; the laws in place across all levels of government; and the way those laws are interpreted and enforced across the city.

Truly ending this crisis will require both intervention and prevention. Over the longer term, it will require a transformation of our city: growing economic opportunities, improving the education of every child, providing more access to mental health support, and so much more. Yet immediately, as this blueprint lays out, we must address the crisis of guns on our streets.

HOW TO SOLVE IT
CITY OF NEW YORK

The residents will do everything in their power as a city to end this crisis. The Adams Administration will enhance NYPD efforts to fight crime with targeted, precision policing that removes guns from our streets; expand the work of the successful anti-violence Crisis Management System, CMS, movement, which addresses the symptoms of gun violence; and bring all New Yorkers together in common cause to work together.

NYPD

In 2021 alone, the NYPD removed more than 6,000 guns off New York City streets. In the first weeks of 2022, officers have already removed 350 illegal guns. The Department will continue to build on this work with the actions outlined below. Yet as detailed later in this report, this challenge cannot be solved by this Department alone. It will require significant action from all levels of government to stop the flow of guns into our city.

Chapter 29

The NYPD will Deepen its Work

Improving existing Public Safety Units with new Neighborhood Safety Teams. Immediately, the NYPD will provide more resources and support.

Public Safety teams in precincts across the five boroughs, which are already playing a significant role in gun removals over the past year.

This additional support includes the creation of Neighborhood Safety Teams, which will focus on gun violence. The city will hold listening to tours in key neighborhoods, truly understanding the challenges of past Anti-Crime Units and providing additional training, supervision, analytics, and risk monitoring to ensure these enhanced teams work with communities.

The Department expects to launch these teams in the next three weeks with a special focus on the 30 precincts where 80% of violence occurs, and has already identified several hundred candidates for these teams.

Putting more Officers on Patrol

After years of efforts to civilianize more roles at the NYPD, this Administration will get it right to better utilize existing resources and place more officers on patrol in key neighborhoods throughout the city. We will go unit by unit to find efficiencies, seek all federal funding available, and aim to have fewer officers on desk and staffing events where they are not needed.

NYPD and State Police
Expanding the partnership between NYPD and State Police

Already, the Adams Administration has launched an expanded partnership between the NYPD and New York State Police. The law enforcement agencies now share critical information, such as license plate records and trace data, as a matter of public policy.

The agencies will also increase the public safety presence around public transportation facilities and create joint strategies to zero-in on illegal guns used in high-intensity drug trafficking areas building on the newly-created gun intelligence task force.

Adding more detection efforts at City entry points for the "Iron Pipeline."

There are no gun manufacturers in New York City. Yet even as the NYPD removed nearly 6,000 last year from our streets, new guns arrived by car, train, and bus every day.

The NYPD will work with State law enforcement to implement spot checks at entry points like Port Authority and other bus and train stations.

NEW YORK STATE
BAIL REFORM

The bail reform legislation passed in 2019 was an attempt at addressing unfairness in our criminal justice system. Years later, our pretrial detention system is still not fixed, and judges do not have the necessary tools they need to protect communities.

New York's bail laws must be fairer, smarter, and more targeted. We must approach pretrial detention through the lens of public safety, something that is not done now.

The Adams Administration will propose a common-sense, targeted set of reforms to strengthen our bail laws to change the law as soon as possible.

Allowing judges to take dangerousness into account. New York is the only state in the country that does not allow a judge to detain a defendant who poses a threat to the community. 49 other states, as well as the federal government, allow judges to consider a defendant's dangerousness.

New York must also meet this common-sense standard. Judges must be able to evaluate a defendant's criminal history and the circumstances of their alleged crime using reasonable criteria to detain those individuals who pose a threat to the safety of the community, especially regarding gun violence.

The power to detain dangerous defendants is not unchecked. A judge must also state his or her reasons for detention on the record, and a defendant must be entitled to a speedy appeal.

<u>Demanding accountability and transparency from our system</u>

Judges' decisions must be public, and their reasons must be stated on the record. There must be full transparency. The public is entitled to full data on how often a judge detains defendants and the race, gender, and age of those detained.

Public, easily accessible data is the check on judges who fail to take a targeted approach towards detention.

These two common-sense, targeted measures would help deliver a pretrial system that is fairer, smarter, and more targeted towards those who would harm our communities and our city.

"Raise The Age"

The Adams Administration fully supports the 2017 New York State legislation to raise the age of criminal responsibility to 18 years old, which amended outdated laws and delivered long-overdue criminal justice reform for our young people.

Yet when it comes to guns, too many New Yorkers in their late teens and early twenties have abused this change, demanding young people under 18 take the fall for guns that are not truly theirs.

The Adams Administration advocates for an amended version for gun arrests:

If a 16- or 17-year-old is arrested on a gun charge, law enforcement should ask the individual where they got the gun. If the individual refuses to disclose that information, prosecutors should have the ability to charge the individual in Criminal Court, rather than Family Court.

The public display of the gun should not be a factor as it is under current legislation: the carrying of a gun should be treated the same way whether the individual displays it or not.

Discovery

Similarly, the 2019 reforms to the discovery process represent a true step forward to make New York City and New York State fairer and more equitable. Yet in the fight against the gun violence, the Adams Administration will advocate for two additional reforms:

Allowing District Attorneys to move forward earlier with gun charges.

We urge the State to pass legislation empowering DAs, in the event of a gun charge, to proceed with Section 30.30 if they have enough evidence to bring to trial, even as they accumulate additional pieces. All evidence would be required to be handed over in discovery 30 days before the trial.

Removing overly burdensome disclosures. The voluminous requirements of the new discovery bill have jammed up too many cases. We urge the State to distinguish what is truly necessary for discovery, especially in cases where a complainant directly brought law enforcement to the scene.

Raising the penalty for gun trafficking.

Currently, an individual receives a Class B felony for selling 10 or more guns in a single year. That number is far too generous to traffickers. We urge New York State legislation that lowers the number to 3 or more guns in a one-year period.

We also urge State legislation to define the possession of 3 or more guns as presumptive evidence of gun trafficking, not merely gun possession.

Working with the Interstate Gun Tracing Consortium.

This week, the Adams Administration will join Governor Hochul's Public Safety team in the first of a series of meetings around gun violence and shared intelligence across all levels of government. We applaud the Governor's focus on these efforts, including the Interstate Gun Tracing Consortium, and will continue to support them in the coming months.

Chapter 30

Off-duty Vermont Sheriff's Deputy Shot

The deputy and a man from Utica, New York, had exchanged gunfire around 3 a.m. Sunday when Saratoga Springs Police ran onto the scene, ordered the deputy to drop his weapon, and shot him several times.

An off-duty sheriff's deputy from Vermont was shot multiple times by police in New York after he was involved in a gunfight with another group of people early Sunday morning, police said.

Shots were fired around 3 a.m. at the intersection of Broadway and Caroline Street in Saratoga Springs, New York, near an area with bars and nightlife, following a scuffle between the deputy and a group of people from the Utica area.

The deputy, who was not identified, was "physically attacked" by at least three people, slammed into the hood of a car and knocked to the ground, Commissioner of Public Safety James Montagnino said during a news conference Sunday.

The deputy picked himself up off the ground and apparently moved his jacket back to show the individuals he was armed. One of the other individuals in the group then drew a handgun and pointed it in the deputy's direction and began firing. The deputy brandished his own handgun, and shots were exchanged, Montagnino said.

Montagnino said he believed seven or eight shots were exchanged in the gunfight, and the deputy shot the Utica man who drew his weapon.

Several Saratoga Springs officers were on duty around the corner on Caroline Street and heard the confrontation and ran to see what was going on. When they did, they saw the deputy "standing on the sidewalk, his gun leveled, and moving from side to side pointing the gun," Montagnino said.

Officials played surveillance footage from a street camera on Broadway and body camera footage from one officer, showing officers repeatedly ordering the deputy to drop the gun and get on the ground.

Montagnino said officers ordered him to drop the gun at least eight times, but the deputy "ignored" the commands.

Montagnino said three officers discharged their weapons, firing a total of 11 shots, resulting in the deputy falling to the ground. The entire incident lasted less than a minute, authorities said.

He said that the deputy suffered 10 bullet wounds, including one to the chest, but the wounds hadn't yet been classified as entry and exit wounds.

"So, it doesn't mean that he was shot 10 times, it simply means that there were 10 wounds. It's certainly possible that he was shot half that number or even less," Montagnino said. "If a bullet penetrated an arm and lodged in the chest, that could be three wounds from one round."

Officers immediately provided aid to an individual who was shot by the deputy and found lying on Broadway, aid to the deputy and to a woman believed to be the deputy's girlfriend who was nicked by one of the bullets in the upper arm, authorities said. All were hospitalized.

Saratoga Springs Sgt. Paul Veitch said Monday that two of the three people injured remain in the hospital in stable condition, and a third victim was released late Sunday. Their names were not released.

Montagnino said it's the first time in nearly 30 years that an on-duty Saratoga Springs officer discharged their weapon.

"Outside of a training exercise, or putting down a rabid animal, this is the first time in 26 years that an officer of the Saratoga Springs Police Department had to discharge a firearm in the line of duty," Montagnino said.

He said the officers involved in the incident would be placed on leave, following standard protocol for officer-involved shootings.

Saratoga Springs Mayor Ron Kim denounced the shooting saying: "Nobody should be on Caroline Street at 3 o'clock in the morning drinking that has a weapon. End of story."

No arrests have been made in the case and New York State Police are investigating the shooting.

Chapter 31

New York City a safe Place to Live

For the most part, New York City is a safe place to live. You just need to stay away from renting or buying properties in dangerous neighborhoods. Theft and burglary are sometimes an issue, but it depends on where you choose to live. Plus, there are plenty of ways to keep your home safe such as using alarm systems.

How safe is Times Square?

Violent crimes aren't a big concern at all. The biggest concern in Times Square is pickpocketing and theft. The large crowds make it easy for people to steal, and thieves can be quite clever with their tactics. This is why you need to carry your belongings in front of you and keep valuables hidden. Never put anything in your back pockets.

Central Park

Central Park is open from six in the morning to one in the morning. While the park is technically open for most of the night, this doesn't mean you should go after dark. The park is almost deserted at night, making you an easy target for crimes, especially if you're alone. Central Park is extremely safe during the day, but nighttime is rather unsafe.

Safety is the responsibility of the whole community.

The NYPD is increasing the number of officers assigned to special school details citywide in response to recent violence near school campuses.

The number of "Youth Coordination Officers" is being boosted to six per precinct, according to a memo Thursday from NYPD Chief of Department Jeffrey Maddrey.

That's a total of 462, up from the original program's goal of 350 across the city. Another NYPD memo, dated Tuesday from Deputy Chief Marlon Larin, calls on School Safety Division officers to step up reporting "when a school incident has the potential for retaliation."

The moves outlined in the memos, which were obtained by Gothamist, follow a spate of recent violence. The Larin memo states that the steps were designed "In order to combat violence at and in the near vicinity" of the city's public schools.

The YCO role was created in 2020 by former Mayor Bill de Blasio and former NYPD Commissioner Dermot Shea with the goal of curbing youth crime. At the time, Shea said the officers would "coordinate with the other cops in the precinct, and with city agencies and local community-service groups that have a stake in improved youth outcomes."

This week, three people were injured in a shooting outside a charter school in Brooklyn. Last month in Queens, a 13-year-old was charged with shooting and wounding two other teens near Campus Magnet High School. Also in January, a 17-year-old boy was chased and stabbed to death after leaving Liberation High School in Coney Island.

Maddrey's memo outlines a series of steps to bolster communications and contacts with school officials, and to ensure that "directed patrols" at schools are completed. Chief of Patrol John M. Chell and Chief of Transit Michael Kemper will oversee the patrols, according to the memo, with Kemper also ensuring that "Transit District School

Safety Teams are being strategically deployed after conferral with their precinct counterpart."

Maddrey also orders precinct commanding officers to meet weekly with school principals, of public as well as private and charter schools; to discuss "issues of note"; and to initiate an "All-Out" that is, redirecting cops on administrative duties into the field to cover dismissals at problematic schools.

In a statement Friday, Department of Education spokesperson Jenna Lyle emphasized the NYPD's role in keeping students safe outside of schools, and highlighted Project Pivot, an initiative launched last year to address school violence, for its part in creating a safe environment for students.

"Safety is the responsibility of the entire community and through Project Pivot we are partnering deeply with the community to engage our students and ensure they are engaged in safe, positive activities in and outside of school," Lyle said. "We appreciate the NYPD for taking this step to ensure our young people are safe when traveling to and from schools, and in their communities."

Chapter 32

Crime Rate in New York City

Crime rates in New York City have been recorded since at least the 1800s. They have spiked ever since the post-war period.

The highest crime totals were recorded in the late 1980s and early 1990s as the crack epidemic surged,[and then declined continuously through the 2000s.

During the 1990s, the New York City Police Department, NYPD, adopted CompStat, broken windows policing, and other strategies in a major effort to reduce crime. The resulting drop in crimes thereafter has been variously attributed to several factors, including the end of the crack epidemic, the increased incarceration rate nationwide, gentrification, an aging population, and the decline of lead poisoning in children.

Organized crime has long been associated with New York City, beginning with the Forty Thieves and the Roach Guards gangs in the Five Points area of Manhattan in the 1820s.

In 1835, the New York Herald was established by James Gordon Bennett, Sr., who helped revolutionize journalism by covering stories that appeal to the masses including crime reporting. When Helen Jewett was murdered on April 10, 1836, Bennett did innovative on-the-scene investigation and reporting and helped bring the story to national attention.

Peter Cooper, at the request of the Common Council, drew up a proposal to create a police force of 1,200 officers. The state legislature approved the proposal on May 7, 1844, and abolished the night watch system.

Under Mayor William Havemeyer, the police force reorganized and officially established itself on May 13, 1845, as the New York Police Department (NYPD). The new system divided the city into three districts and set up courts, magistrates, clerks, and station houses.

New York Gangs

Originally based in New York's Lower East Side, the Forty Thieves gang was formed in 1825 by Edward Coleman.

Initially it was formed to rebel against their low social status, but the members soon turned to crime to relieve their frustration. This gang emerged due to prejudice and class distinction.

Such social conditions were evident in the Five Points area of New York in the 1820s. Canal Street, the Bowery, Broadway, and Mulberry Street bordered this area, which was a slum infested with mosquitoes and disease.

The Forty Thieves met at a Centre Street grocery store owned by Rosanna Peers, a notorious fence of stolen goods who also sold illegal alcohol in an underground speakeasy.

At Peers' grocery gang members would be given assignments and issued strict quotas on the gang's share of illegal activities. The quota system proved a great motivator among veterans competing against younger members seeking to take older members' positions.

However, in the long term the gang was unable to maintain internal discipline in early New York, and by 1850 the gang had dissolved with its members joining larger gangs or leaving on their own.

From the violence to the high crime rates, Five Points desperately lacked the aid of government support. The Forty Thieves saw this as an economic opportunity, as they established relations with Tammany Hall.

This corrupt bureaucracy provided community services in exchange for money and support from its residents to fund their corrupt agendas. The juvenile Little Forty Thieves, an apprentice street gang of the original Forty Thieves, would outlast their mentors, continuing to commit illegal activities throughout the 1850s before eventually joining the later street gangs following the American Civil War in 1865.

Today in New York, the most prominent New York City gangs are Bloods, Crips, Latin Kings, Nietas, Five Prisoners, Silenciosos, Matatones, Rat Hunters, and Zulu Nation. They are groups that span ethnicity, race, and neighborhoods.

Chapter 33

NYC Gangsters

Lucky Luciano

Charles "Lucky" Luciano was an Italian American mobster, was considered the founder and father of organized crime in America. He was the most powerful Mafia boss of all time.

Luciano split power between Five Families. The Bonanno, Colombo, Gambino, Genovese, and Lucchese. This was a power sharing arrangement known as The Commission to avoid the type of bloody wars he fought to put himself into power.

Paul Kelly

Paul Kelly was an Italian immigrant who founded the Five Points Gang in New York City. It was one of the last major street gangs in late 19th century New York and was the producing ground for many future criminals including Lucky Luciano and Bugsy Siegel.

Big Jack Zelig

Big Jack Zelig was a pickpocket and thief who eventually became the leader of the Eastman gang and was a mentor to Murder Inc head

Louis Buchalter. He was shot to prevent him from testifying against his own gang in 1908. He was 24 years old at the time.

Monk Eastman

He was the founder of the Eastman Gang, one of the most powerful NYC street gangs at the turn of the 20th century. He served five years in Sing Sing for robbery and served in the US military during World War One. He was shot to death in 1920.

Benjamin Siegel

He is known as Bugsy. Bugsy was a gangster associated with Lucky Luciano. He was also a member of Murder Inc and after moving out of New York. He was also the prime mover behind developing the Las Vegas Strip. He was killed in 1947.

Arnold Rothstein

He was a New York mob kingpin at the turn of the 20th century. He was also known as "The Brain". There was a rumor that he fixed the 1919 World Series. He is regarded to be the person who transformed organized crime into a business. He was murdered in 1928.

Meyer Lansky

He was a longtime partner of Lucky Luciano, was one of the most powerful criminals in the United States. Known as an accountant for the mob, his criminal specialty was gambling. He established casinos worldwide including in Las Vegas and Cuba. He was never convicted on charges more serious than illegal gambling and died of lung cancer in 1982.

Dutch Schultz was a New York City gangster who made his fortune in bootlegging. He was a particular target of prosecutor Thomas Dewey. In 1935 when Schultz attempted to kill Dewey against the orders of the Five Families, he was killed.

Louis "Lepke" Buchalter was one of the heads of Murder Inc in the 1920s and 1930s as well as a labor racketeer. He was convicted of murder and put to death in the electric chair at Sing Sing in 1944. He is the only mob boss to be put to death in the United States.

Tammany Hall was a New York City political organization that functioned from 1786 to 1960. It was a political machine for the Democratic Party that helped control New York City and State including party nominations and patronage. The most famous period of Tammany Hall was when it was under the control of William M. Tweed, also known as "Boss," Tweed.

James Joseph Hines

Jimmy Hines was the most powerful Tammany Hall boss in the 1930s and 1940s, ruling out of Manhattan's Eleventh Assembly District. He had close ties to mobster Lucky Luciano and Gangster "Dutch" Schultz. He was convicted on convicted on 13 counts of racketeering and served five years in jail.

Jimmy Coonan was a Manhattan based mobster who was leader of the Westies gang, the last major Irish gang in the area, in the 1960s and 1970s. Coonan was sentenced to 75 years in prison for racketeering in 1988.

Gotti

Gotti, also known as "The Dapper Don," for his expensive clothes and "The Teflon Don" for his acquittal in three high-profile trials in the 1980s was head of the Gambino crime family.

He came to power through the assassination of Paul Castellano in 1985. In 1992, Gotti was convicted of five murders, conspiracy to commit murder, racketeering, obstruction of justice, illegal gambling, extortion, tax evasion, and loansharking. He was sentenced to life in prison without parole and died of throat cancer in 2002.

The Five Points was a Manhattan neighborhood that is today covered by the Civic Center, the collective name for the city, state and federal administration buildings and courthouses located in Manhattan, Columbus Park, Foley Square, and NYC Department of Corrections facilities.

During a major part of the 19th century, this neighborhood was known as a crime-ridden slum controlled by a multitude of gangs and as a breeding ground for criminals. Its reputation was in part the reason the city eventually demolished the place.

Chapter 34

The Cause of Crime Wave

On December 31, 2020, a 40-year-old man named Leon Casiquito walked into Kelly Liquors on Route 66 in Albuquerque and tried to shoplift a bottle of tequila.

When one of the owners, Danny Choi, tried to stop him, Casiquito flashed a small pocketknife. Choi told police he knocked the bottle out of Casiquito's hand with a stick and Casiquito left the store.

Choi locked the door, but Casiquito hung around in the parking lot, shouting that he was going to beat up the store's employees. One of them called the police, and soon four officers arrived and wrestled Casiquito to the ground.

He was charged with armed robbery and aggravated assault with a deadly weapon, despite not actually attacking anyone with the pocketknife, and held without bail at the Metropolitan Detention Center in Albuquerque.

Casiquito's Case

Casiquito had had similar run-ins with law enforcement before, mostly related to his troubles with alcohol and drugs. Those problems, his family believes, may have started with the pills he was prescribed in his teens after he was hit by a car while riding a four-wheeler and thrown 30 feet, putting him into a coma for a few days.

At 30, he suffered another accident when a car hit him while he was out walking, breaking both his legs, and requiring more pain medication.

By the time of his 2020 arrest, his family thought that a brief break in jail, which is what someone in Casiquito's situation could expect under normal circumstances, might help him get himself clean.

But these were not normal circumstances. Like many states, New Mexico had drastically curtailed the operation of its courts in response to the pandemic.

Some civil trials and preliminary hearings for criminal matters moved online, but actual criminal trials needed to be conducted in person in front of juries. Bernalillo County, which includes Albuquerque, suspended such trials for much of 2020 and 2021.

Meanwhile, new cases kept pouring in, partly because of the surge in violent crime that accompanied the pandemic. The nation's homicide rate rose by nearly 30 percent in 2020 and another 5 percent in 2021, essentially erasing two decades' worth of declines in deadly violence.

Criminologists have offered several explanations for the increase, including the rise in gun sales early in the pandemic, changes in police behavior following the protests over the murder of George Floyd, and the social disruptions caused by closures of schools and interruptions in social services.

But many people who work in criminal justice are zeroing in on another possible factor, the extended shutdown of so much of the court system, the institution at the heart of public order.

This could have led to more violence in several ways. Prosecutors confronted with a growing volume of cases decided not to act against certain suspects, who went on to commit other crimes. Victims or witnesses became less willing to testify as time passed and their memories of events grew foggy, weakening cases against perpetrators.

The suspects were denied substance-abuse treatment or other services that they would normally have accessed through the criminal-justice system, with dangerous consequences.

Above all, experts say, the shutdowns undermined the promise that crimes would be promptly punished. The theory that "swift, certain, and fair" consequences deter crimes is credited to the late criminologist Mark Kleiman.

The idea is that it's the speed of repercussions, rather than their severity, that matters most. By putting the justice system on hold for so long, many jurisdictions weakened that effect. In some cases, people were left to seek street justice in the absence of institutional justice.

As Regan Cunningham, a senior partner at the California Partnership for Safe Communities, put it, closing courts sent "a message that there are no consequences, and there is no help."

Many courts around the country still aren't operating at full capacity, and law-and-order types aren't the only ones concerned. Defense attorneys and members of the progressive prosecutor movement are worried too.

The Sixth Amendment guarantees defendants a speedy trial, but many have been sitting in jail for months on end. "A lot of the Constitution has been kind of glossed over," Doug Wilber, a public defender in Albuquerque, told me.

Chapter 35

How to Build a Life

Goering and O'Connor tried to make the restart as palatable as possible. Judges with health concerns were exempted from jury trials. Citizens called for jury duty were told they could opt out if they had concerns about catching the coronavirus.

O'Connor gave a local hospital administrator his cellphone number in case any hospital staff were called as potential jurors, saying that he would make sure to waive them.

These steps raised a different concern among some defense lawyers: that the jurors would be pandemic-dismissing hang-'em-high types. But that turned out not to be the case. The initial batch of cases resulted in an unusually high rate of acquittals.

"I don't have any problem with any of these juries," a defense lawyer, Bradley Sylvester, who worked on some of those cases, told me. "I had a lot of faith in the jury system."

There were wrinkles to iron out. Some lawyers asked for and received exceptions to the courtroom mask mandate during jury selection, so they could see potential jurors' faces as they answered questions.

The plexiglass could be tricky to see through if the light hit it at certain angles. One juror had to be replaced after he tested positive for COVID. But the judges said they knew of no serious illnesses traced to the court.

By the end of 2020, homicides were up sharply in Wichita, as elsewhere, thanks in large part to the early-summer shooting spike that had motivated the court reopening. But the court was ready to process those cases.

In January 2021 it expanded its list of jury trials to include murder cases and other major felonies. Overall, it managed to hold 32 criminal jury trials in 2020, compared with 75 in 2019 a much smaller drop than the ones in Albuquerque and other cities. "It's important for the community to see the courts functioning," said O'Connor. And in Wichita, they did.

Albuquerque had struggled with court backlogs and jail overcrowding long before the pandemic. In the mid-1990s, inmates at the city's Metropolitan Detention Center filed a federal class-action lawsuit over the crowded conditions, and it remained in litigation for two decades before being settled.

In 2019, the district attorney's office put out a glossy report that stressed the importance of accelerating the workings of the criminal-justice system. "Speed is the best deterrent," the report stated. "Through continually improved processes to swiftly intervene by initiating cases quickly, we are seeing a sustained drop in crime."

Accompanying this was a graph showing a sharp decline in overall crime since 2017.

But then came the pandemic and the courthouse closures. The New Mexico Supreme Court suspended jury trials from March to July 2020, restarted them with strict limits that summer, then shut them down again from November 2020 to February 2021. Instead of grand juries, the district attorney's office had to rely on preliminary hearings, held largely online, to initiate cases.

This complicated matters, because New Mexico's stricter evidentiary rules for such hearings meant that lawyers had to get defendants and witnesses to show up, almost like a mini trial. In many instances they didn't, making it impossible to move forward. The number of new cases fell dramatically.

In 2019, the county initiated about 3,700 cases; in 2020 and 2021, the number plunged to about 2,300. And very few of these made it to trial.

Last year, the resumption of court operations happened so haltingly that the county held only 29 criminal jury trials, two-thirds less than in 2019.

For Adolfo Mendez, the chief of policy and planning for the district attorney's office, the consequence of this falloff was plain. A person charged with a crime, he told me, "Doesn't see any consequence of it. They're released back into the community."

In Albuquerque, as elsewhere, the new constraints worried defense lawyers too. Wilber, the public defender, was concerned about the "dehumanizing" effect of defendants having to appear remotely, over Zoom, for their preliminary examinations or detention hearings.

When defendants appeared on a video feed from jail, he feared, judges were more inclined to keep them there. "It's human nature: It's easy to remain with the default," he told me. "They're already sitting in jail, so why not just stay there?"

Wilber also worried about how COVID restrictions limited defendants' access to their lawyers, and that the backlogs were giving judges and prosecutors an excuse to push past due-process protections once cases finally did get to the front of the line, to keep things moving as fast as possible.

"At first, it was about safety and public health," he said of the backlog, "but from our angle, it started to feel like an excuse, an easy way to do away with a lot of protections."

Meanwhile, defense lawyers were hearing from their clients about the worsening conditions at the jail. Reporting by the Albuquerque Journal revealed just how dire things had become.

By late 2021, the jail was short about 150 officers, a vacancy rate of more than 30 percent.

The jail's then-chief told the Journal that the administration was taking various steps to improve officer morale and recruiting. At the time of Casiquito's death, the corrections officer on that pod was overseeing 64 cells, double the normal purview. "It's like a medieval Turkish prison," Wilber told me.

As the nationwide homicide rate continued to increase in 2021, Wichita managed to buck the trend: Homicides there declined that year, to 54, a drop of 9 percent from the year before. Countless factors probably contributed, but local officials are convinced that their ability to get the courts running played a role.

In addition to resuming jury trials, the county has taken other steps to reduce its backlog. Last October, it summoned back a quartet of retired judges to head up what it called the "ARPA Court," because the judges were paid for by funds from the federal American Rescue Plan Act.

With their help, the county held 54 criminal jury trials last year, only 28 percent less than in 2019. This year, it's roughly on track to return to its pre-pandemic pace.

On one recent weekday, the Wichita courthouse was buzzing. In O'Connor's courtroom, the plexiglass dividers were stacked in a pile, awaiting removal. The judge was presiding over a sentencing hearing for a man convicted of murder in the July 2019 shooting of a 20-year-old Air Force member outside a party. "

The victim's family had come from South Carolina, and his father gave a wrenching testimonial about the loss of his son.

Afterward, in his chambers, O'Connor said this was another reason to get court operations moving again: to provide grieving family members with some closure. "You see just how important it is for family members to come to court," he told me.

In another courtroom, a jury trial was under way for a 2021 domestic-violence-assault charge. Goering, sitting nearby in his chambers under the Hendrix and Joplin posters, said he was relieved to see just how close to normal the court was functioning.

"We were going to have a backlog no matter what," he said. "But I was just determined that it was going to be as small as possible."

Over the past few months, I've visited a few cities where the courts underwent some of the country's longest suspensions, and I found a very different scene.

In Oakland, California, where jury trials started resuming only in the spring of 2021, the Alameda County Superior Courthouse still seemed frozen at the peak of the pandemic, with signs ordering visitors to take staircases only in certain directions and jurors and courtroom personnel still in mandatory masks.

In an interview in late April, the district attorney, Nancy O'Malley, told me that the county had about 4,700 felony cases and 6,000 misdemeanor cases pending with a future court date, up by a third from before the pandemic began. "The court is still not fully operational," she said.

She wasn't sure if the county could have done differently, given California's strict edicts on social distancing. "With rules for six feet apart, there was no way you could have people sitting in a box made for 12 people," she said. "I don't know how you do it while keeping people healthy."

But she had little doubt that the court constraints had played a role in the rise in crime in Oakland, which last year saw homicides jump to 134, its highest tally since 2006. The absence or delay of consequences for many offenders created the perception of a "lawless society," she told me.

In Seattle, the backlog of felony cases in the King County Superior Court stood at 4,800 in May, about 50 percent above pre-pandemic averages, after the court repeatedly suspended jury trials, including early this year, during the spread of the Omicron variant. Seattle has also experienced a sharp rise in violent crime. The number of shootings last year, both fatal and nonfatal, was up 78 percent over 2019.

While I was there, I spoke with the director of the county's Department of Public Defense, Anita Khandelwal, who offered a contrary view: She said that the solution to the backlogs was not simply to try to push through as many cases as quickly as possible.

Prosecutors, she said, should rethink whether it was necessary to bring so many cases in the first place, and should distract more people accused of nonviolent crimes into alternative, community-based resolution programs.

Back in Albuquerque, Mendez, in the district attorney's office, said he could see the case for such rethinking, but legislators would have to take that on.

For his office, the immediate challenge remained working through a backlog that now had prosecutors facing a typical caseload of 80 felonies each, up from 50 pre-pandemic.

When I visited the Bernalillo County Courthouse and the nearby Metropolitan Court in April, many proceedings remained online, and the buildings were eerily still. One would not have guessed that the county was groaning under a pile of untried cases.

The costs of the delays were not hard to discern, though. In one trial, on charges of criminal sexual penetration of a minor in 2014, the defendant's father struggled to recall his responses to attorneys' questions in 2018. It had, after all, been four years.

Still, the state and local courts defend the approach they took. "In developing public health safeguards and operating procedures for courthouses during the pandemic, members of the Supreme Court monitored COVID conditions in New Mexico, consulted with state health officials and regularly convened virtual meetings of chief judges across the state," wrote Barry Massey, a spokesperson for the state's Supreme Court, in a statement. And a spokesperson for the county-court system said it was simply following the Supreme Court's protocols.

Leon Casiquito's family has filed a wrongful-death lawsuit against both the county and the company that provides the jail's medical services.

The defendants have denied most of the allegations and moved to have the case dismissed. The law firm handling the suit is well acquainted with the costs of the extended court hiatus; two of its other clients were found not guilty in murder cases, both on claims of self-defense, but had to sit in jail for a year longer than typical before their trials. The Casiquitos' case is still in the discovery phase, but the family's lawyers expect that the trial will be delayed.

Casiquito's older half-brother, Erik Fisher, who helped raise him, visits Casiquito's grave almost every day and calls his mother to console her. "Leon was her baby," he told me. "They were very close. She took it really, hard."

Out on Route 66, the man who chased Casiquito out of Kelly's Liquors, Danny Choi, was unaware of what exactly had become of him. Choi had gotten a call from the district attorney's office telling him only that the case had been closed.

"I asked the prosecutor what happened, and he said he died," Choi said. "He didn't tell me how."

Leon Casiquito's case had been categorized as "track one," meaning it was supposed to be heard within six months. But by the time that deadline rolled around in the spring of 2021, Bernalillo County had fallen far behind schedule.

The Second Judicial District Court had held 86 criminal jury trials in 2019. In 2020, that tally plunged to 18.

Casiquito had spent almost six months in jail when, on June 29, 2021, a district judge issued an order postponing his case indefinitely.

During daily calls to his mother, he described how jail conditions were worsening, his half-brother told me. The inmate population was growing, and the jail was short on staff.

Inmates were frequently placed on lockdown and confined to their cells for virtually the entire day.

Casiquito was spending all that time locked in with his cellmate, Telea Lui, who had schizophrenia and had been charged with aggravated battery after attacking his mother with a 20-pound dumbbell.

On the evening of October 25, Lui flew into a rage, punching and kicking Casiquito for such a long time more than 20 minutes that, as Lui later told officers, he had to pause to catch his breath and get a drink of water.

Inmates in nearby cells called for help, but no guards were nearby....

By the time correctional officers finally entered the cell, Casiquito was not breathing, and had "severe trauma" to the head. They pronounced him dead.

Lui's lawyer would later state that Lui was defending himself against Casiquito, who he said had been "hitting him in the legs in a nagging manner."

Lui has since been found dangerous and incompetent to stand trial and has been referred to a state psychiatric hospital.

It had been nearly 10 months since Casiquito was arrested for trying to steal a bottle of tequila with a pocketknife. His death was one of 116 homicides in Albuquerque in 2021, by far the most the city had ever recorded in a single year.

Six hundred miles east of Albuquerque, in Wichita, Kansas, authorities had worried from early in the pandemic about the effect of closing courtrooms. They decided to do something about it.

Violence had surged in the spring and early summer of 2020, as it had in so many other cities. Wichita police saw a sharp rise in drive-by shootings. And officials noticed something else, said then, police chief Gordon Ramsay.

Many suspects arrested in the shootings were defiant, suggesting that nothing would come of the charges against them because the pandemic had shut down most of the court system. Defendants were, as a result, disinclined to take a plea deal. Why plead guilty to avoid a trial when no trials were happening anyway?

Ramsay contacted the Sedgwick County district attorney and others about the need to get the system back on track as soon as possible. He found allies in the county's chief judge, Jeffrey Goering, and in Kevin O'Connor, the presiding judge of the court's criminal department.

"The option of just having cases pile up in high-volume dockets was not an option at all," Goering told me. "If that meant thinking outside the box, that's what it meant."

After consultations with the county health director, the county courthouse resumed jury trials in July 2020, just four months after having suspended them.

It got creative. It spent more than $30,000 to outfit its two largest courtrooms with plexiglass dividers and set up a big tent outside.

At first, it called only less serious cases, because lawyers got fewer peremptory strikes to use in jury selection for those cases, which meant that juries could be selected from smaller candidate pools.

Wichita judges were adamant that the move to reopen was not intended as some sort of political statement, prioritizing prosecutions over public health. Goering himself hardly fits the red-state law-and-order stereotype: He studied philosophy in college and has decorated his chambers with homages to Jimi Hendrix and Janis Joplin.

With his beard and shaggy hair, he bears an uncanny resemblance to his cinematic hero, the Dude from The Big Lebowski. Getting trials going again was a pure civic reflex, he told me. "I took the opinion that the cost to society was greater from the consequences of not moving these cases and keeping the courtroom locked down too long than from an outbreak of COVID," he said.

Chapter 36

Richmond, California sees ATM Crime Wave

The Richmond, California police department has seen an increase in smash-and-grab robberies against ATM users. With this technique, after a customer withdraws cash from an ATM.

The thieves watch where they place the money, then they smash the car window and grab the purse or wallet with the cash and flee the scene, according to a report by Kron 4.

The thieves have at times followed the victims for several blocks from the bank, waiting for them to stop at a red light before moving in to smash the car window.

Police recommend citizens lock their vehicles, don't sit in your vehicle upon completing the ATM withdraw.

The residents were informed to secure their purse in a trunk or locked glove box, according to the report.

Chapter 37

Youth Gangs

Once considered an urban problem, gang violence has spread to smaller cities, towns, and rural areas.

There are more than 24,500 different youth gangs around the country, with more than 772,500 teenage and young adult members.

A gang is defined as a group of people who engage in joint violent, illegal, or criminal activity.

Gangs usually identify themselves with a common name and symbol. Research has estimated that teenagers who are gang members are more likely to commit serious and violent crimes and are more likely to be victims of homicide than non-gang members.

There has been a steep increase in gang activity in the United States since the 1970's, but since 1996 gang membership has decreased except in cities with populations of over 25,000. The average age of gang members is around 17 to 18 years.

Approximately half of all gang members are 18 or older; these older gang members are much more likely to be involved in serious and violent crimes. Females are less likely to be involved with gangs than males, however, one 11- city survey of eighth graders found that 38 percent of gang members were female.

Further research has shown that 78 percent of female gang members have been involved in gang fights and 39 percent have attacked someone with a weapon.

Teenagers join gangs for many reasons, including excitement and a sense of belonging. Suggestions are offered for keeping teenagers away from gangs, such as finding positive ways to spend time, avoiding gang members, and not carrying weapons.

Chapter 38

Violent Crimes in Different Cities

I f you had to guess which town in the United States was the single most violent, would you have picked California?

Probably not....

Most of us would likely name St. Louis or Baltimore, maybe Chicago or even New York.

A few, if any, would point to the 204-person Industry, a suburb about 22 miles away from downtown Los Angeles. But, according to the most recent federal crime statistics, Industry's rate of violent crime is an astonishing 35,784.31 per 100,000 people, nearly 10,000% higher than the overall U.S. violent crime rate.

The FBI reported that a total of 73 violent crimes took place in Industry in 2017, 1 murder, 5 rapes, 36 robberies and 31 aggravated assaults. With the city's tiny population, that makes for an eye-popping crime rate.

In addition to the tiny population, digging into the city's economy reveals why Industry's crime rate is so high. It's almost entirely industrial. There are 15 times more companies in Industry than people.

Basically, the crime rate is so high because nobody lives there.

It's not fair to call Industry the most violent or dangerous city in the country. Then which one is? Let's examine which cities are most dangerous and break down which violent crimes are most prevalent in which cities.

All Violent Crimes

The FBI's annual Crime in the U.S. reports reveal all sorts of details about the state of crime in our country and include details on crimes committed, people arrested, weapons used and more.

For our purposes, we're focusing on which cities have the highest rates of violent crimes. Murder, aggravated assault, rape, and robbery. We're also excluding all cities under 10,000 in population; sorry, Industry.

Among the cities that remain, examining the total number of violent crimes produces a list along the lines of what you might expect, with all four of the 2 million+ cities coming in at Nos. 1-4 on the list, but two relatively small cities, Indianapolis, and Baltimore, seem to be punching above their weight class.

Across the entire U.S. in 2017, about 1.3 million violent crimes took place.

Of the top 10 cities, six of them have populations over 1 million, while Baltimore has the lowest population among the top 10. The inverse of this list is a little bit trickier, as many communities had no reported violent crimes at all and far more had only a few.

As we know, though, just looking at sheer numbers tells only one part of the story. A better comparison takes into account population differences, so which cities have the highest rates of violent crimes relative to their population size?

The U.S. city with the single highest population-adjusted rate of violent crime is Anniston, Alabama, a community of about 22,000 in the northeastern part of the state. Another Alabama community, Bessemer, is No. 2, and three others in the state are among the top 25.

Several large cities are on the list, including St. Louis, Detroit, Memphis, Kansas City and Baltimore, which also appeared on the list of cities with the highest numbers of violent crimes.

Murder

Just over 17,000 people were the victims of murder or intentional manslaughter in the United States in 2017, making murder one of the few violent crimes that's actually rising. Since 2014, the number of murders in the U.S. has gone up by more than 22% and stands at levels last seen more than a decade ago.

Chicago had the most murders among all cities with 653, nearly double the second-highest city, Baltimore.

East St. Louis, No. 4 on our violent-crime rate list, tops the list of cities by murder rate, with a rate that's far higher than the next couple of cities on the list, Chester, Pennsylvania, and Vinita Park, Missouri. Several major cities are on this list, including St. Louis, Baltimore, Detroit, and New Orleans.

Rape

An estimated 135,755 rapes took place in the U.S. in 2017, though rape is a crime that's notoriously underreported and tragically misunderstood. Even in an era where there are fruitful conversations taking place about sexual consent, the states don't agree on what constitutes rape, with some jurisdictions seeming to use a definition that would exclude things like date rape.

More rapes were reported in Los Angeles than any other city, though New York City was close.

While the top of this list generally falls in line with population size, there are some interesting entries here. Columbus and Austin both have less than 1 million residents, though they are Nos. 9 and 10, respectively. Notably, both cities are home to two of the 10 largest public college campuses in the country, Ohio State University, and the University of Texas. An estimated 1 in 10 college students will experience rape or sexual assault.

After accounting for population differences, our list changes dramatically. In fact, only three of the cities among the top 25 have populations of over 1 million.

Cadillac, a city of just over 10,000 in northwestern Michigan has the nation's highest population-adjusted rape rate, posting a rate that's about one-third higher than the next-highest, another Michigan city, Alpena. Texas and Michigan both have five cities in the top 25, while Colorado, South Carolina, and Utah each have two. Salt Lake City, at No. 25, is the largest one on the list, with a population just 2 million.

Robbery

The second-most common violent crime, robbery, is often confused with property crimes like burglary or larceny, but while precise definitions can vary by jurisdiction, robbery is marked by one key difference violence or the threat of force.

More than 300,000 robberies took place in the U.S. in 2017, with large cities generally accounting for large numbers of such incidents.

New York had by far the most robberies reported, which makes sense if you accept that the archetypal crime in the city is mugging, which is a form of robbery. A handful of smaller cities, Baltimore, Indianapolis, and Memphis leapfrogged some larger ones to rise to the top 10.

After accounting for differences in population, the city with the highest robbery rate is Baltimore, which followers of the public dispute between President Donald Trump and U.S. Rep. Elijah Cummings would likely not find surprising.

Six New Jersey cities are in the top 25, the most of any state, while Florida has three and California, Georgia, Ohio, and Pennsylvania have two each. No city in the top 25 has a total population exceeding 750,000.

<u>Aggravated Assault</u>

By far the most common violent crime in the U.S., accounting for more than all the others combined, is aggravated assault.

This is not the only type of assault crime, however, and what distinguishes aggravated assault from other forms, such as simple assault, is the use of a weapon or the infliction of serious bodily injury on the victim.

More than 810,000 aggravated assaults were reported in the U.S. in 2017, which represents an increase from the previous year, though the number has fallen by nearly 17% since 1998.

According to sheer volume, New York had far and away the highest number of aggravated assaults, and the remainder of the top 10 mostly includes heavily populated cities.

Texas is the only state with more than one city among the top 10, but New York's nearly 30,000 aggravated assaults accounted for more than Houston and San Antonio combined.

Anniston, Alabama, which had the highest overall violent crime rate, also tops this list, along with four other Alabama cities. Michigan and Louisiana each have three, and two cities with the same name appear Camden, one in New Jersey and the other in Arkansas with nearly identical rates.

<u>25 Most Dangerous U.S. Cities</u>

So which cities are all-around the most dangerous? There's one aspect we haven't addressed here, and that's how these cities rate relative to the overall rates of crime in the U.S.

To figure out the 25 most dangerous American cities, we've also considered national rates of murder, rape, robbery and aggravated assault, calculating each city's crime rate as a percentage of the corresponding U.S. rate and then averaging the four percentages together.

If you've read closely to this point, you probably could have guessed more than a few of these, but there are some interesting entries.

Our analysis finds the single most dangerous American city is East St. Louis, Illinois, just on the other side of the Mississippi River from St. Louis, Missouri, which is No. 5 on our list.

All 25 have appeared on at least one of the lists of the population-adjusted crime rates, and most have appeared multiple times.

Detroit is the largest city in the top 25, and you may be wondering how safe America's largest cities are. Among the 35 or so cities on our list with populations that exceed 500,000, Baltimore is by far the most dangerous, according to the city's violent crime rates as a percentage of corresponding rates for the entire U.S.

Only three of the 30+ largest U.S. cities have crime rates that average out to less than 100% of the respective crime rates for the nation, and most of them have rates in excess of 200% of the national rates.

In Conclusion

What we haven't introduced here is the way of city violence. To be sure, total population plays a role, though when compared to overall U.S. crime rates, the largest city in the country, New York City, has one of the lowest incidents of crime relative to the nation.

It's a fact that FBI data indicates violent crime is a bigger problem in Baltimore than in any other major city. But Baltimore is not unique in having high rates of crime, as most of the largest American cities have similarly high rates of crime.

Those communities, places like Albuquerque and Indianapolis and Milwaukee and Phoenix, are rarely ever held up as examples of failing cities by politicians who want to pick fights.

We're not suggesting we have the answers for how to improve the lives of people in Baltimore and make them less likely to be victimized by violence. But we do know that improvements are possible, as violent crime, and crime in general, is becoming less common across the United States.

A good place to start would be remembering that "real America" is urban America the 9,000-plus cities we examined accounted for nearly two-thirds of the entire U.S. population.

About This Story

All the crime data used came from the FBI's 2017 Crime in the United States report, which was published in 2018. This is the most recent dataset that federal officials have released. They used information on offenses known to law enforcement sorted by the city.

The FBI also sorts data by metropolitan statistical areas, but wanted to use the most granular data possible, so, it was opted for cities proper. There are a few limitations to this data, most notably that the state of North Carolina does not conform to the FBI's definition of rape, so that information was not available for cities in that state.

References

1. "Offenses Known to Law Enforcement by State by City, 2017". FBI. Retrieved February 16, 2019.
2. "Crime Rankings 2011-2012". CQ Press.
3. "Table 08, Data Declaration - Crime in the United States 2019". Fbi.gov. Retrieved April 18, 2022.
4. "Caution Against Ranking". FBI. Retrieved August 8, 2012.
5. "A Word About UCR Data". FBI. Archived from the original on September 23, 2010. Retrieved October 12, 2010.
6. Criminologists Condemn City crime rankings (November 16, 2008).PRNewswire. Retrieved January 13, 2008.
7. Oliveira, M. "More crime in cities? On the scaling laws of crime and the inadequacy of per capita rankings—a cross-country study". Crime
8. Science. 10: 27. doi:10.1186/s40163-021-00155-8.
9. Boivin, R. "On the use of crime rates". Canadian Journal of Criminology and Criminal Justice. 55(2): 263–277. doi:10.3138/cjccj.2012-E-06.

About the Author

Norma Iris Pagan Morales was born in Ponce, Puerto Rico. She comes from a very lovable family. Her parents, Juan Jose Pagan Rodriguez, and Digna Morales Figueroa, now deceased, always helped her with her projects as a writer and teaching career. Norma had three siblings, Adelin Milagros Pagan Morales, Juan Jose Pagan Morales, and Julio Manuel Pagan Morales. Julio Manuel Pagan Morales died on September 19, 1998, and Adelin Milagros Pagan Morales died on February 17, 2023.

Norma did all her academic studies in New York City, Puerto Rico, and Canada. She worked in the City of New York Police Department. As an Educator, she worked in New York City Bd. of Education as an English Teacher, in Puerto Rico Bd. of Education as an English teacher and in the Puerto Rico Army National.

Norma has published twelve books: Proud of My Puerto Rican Bequest, ¿Porque Soy Boricua? Poemas del Alma, Art in Written Form, A Baffling Short Stories Collection, On Job in the Big Apple, Puerto Rican Soldiers Serving with Pride, Nature's Rage in the Caribbean, Boricua de Pura Cepa, You are the One, The Unfaithfuls and Christopher Columbus

www.ingramcontent.com/pod-product-compliance
Lightning Source LLC
Chambersburg PA
CBHW021624120626
46545CB00002B/380